R.I.P.

Artist include:

Greg Christian
Jason Brooks
Martin LaCasse
Jeff Zuck
Bryan Randolph
Jef Wright
Eric Thrice
Dave Fox
Mario Desa
Chris Trevino
Aaron Coleman
Casey Cokrlic
Hudge
Lee Hanna
BJ Betts
Jason Freeman
Matt Shamah
Gradey Spades
Claudia Baca
Flip
Cory Lenherr
Derrick Snodgrass
Zack Kinsey
Rex Barnes
Grez
Rob Hiestand
Adam Ciferri
Luke Stewart
Isaac Fainkujen
Mike Roper
Jared Isenberg
Mike Dorsey
Kurt Melancon
Jason Loui
Kore Flatmo
Mike Davis

R.I.P. was originally published in 2004

Wolf Wizard Press© would like to thank everyone who helped in the making of R.I.P.; Greg Christian, Jason Brooks, Martin LaCasse, Jeff Zuck, Dave Fox, Mario Desa, Chris Trevino, Aaron Coleman, Casey Cokrlic, Hudge, Lee Hanna, Matt Shamah, Claudia Baca, Flip, Cory Lenherr, BJ Betts, Derrick Snodgrass, Adam Ciferri, Mike Davis, Zack Kinsey, Rex Barnes, Jared Isenberg, Rob Hiestand, Kevin Cox, Luke Stewart, Mike Roper, Isaac Fainkujen, Grez, Mike Dorsey, Kurt Melancon, Jason Loui, Kore Flatmo, Jef Wright, Eric Thrice, Bryan Randolph, Grady Spades, Sara Dyer, Tiffany Allen and Tim Azinger.

Note* *Please only use this book as a reference to inspire ideas and* **do not copy** *and tattoo these images.*

Wolf Wizard Press©
150 Ridge Street
Reno, NV 89509

R.I.P. Volume One Copyright 2004©

Edited by: Jason Freeman

jfreemantattoo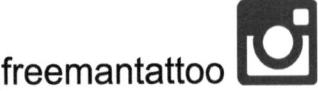

Made in the USA.

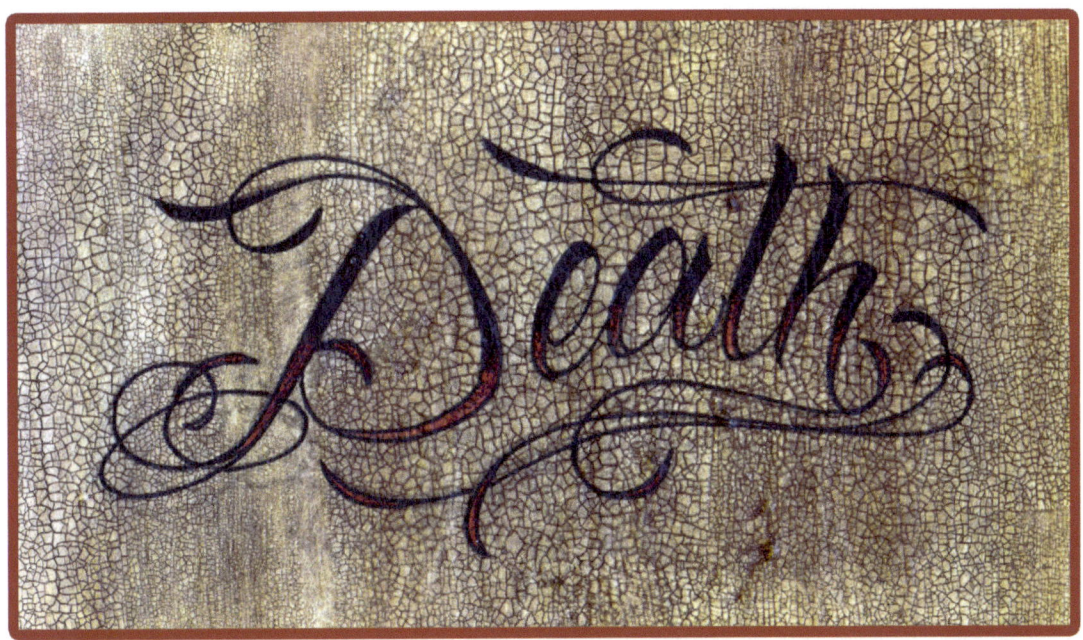

Kevin Cox

Greg Christian

252 Tattoo 24525 Sprague Rd. Columbia Station, OH 44028
(440)235-6699
www.252tattoo.com

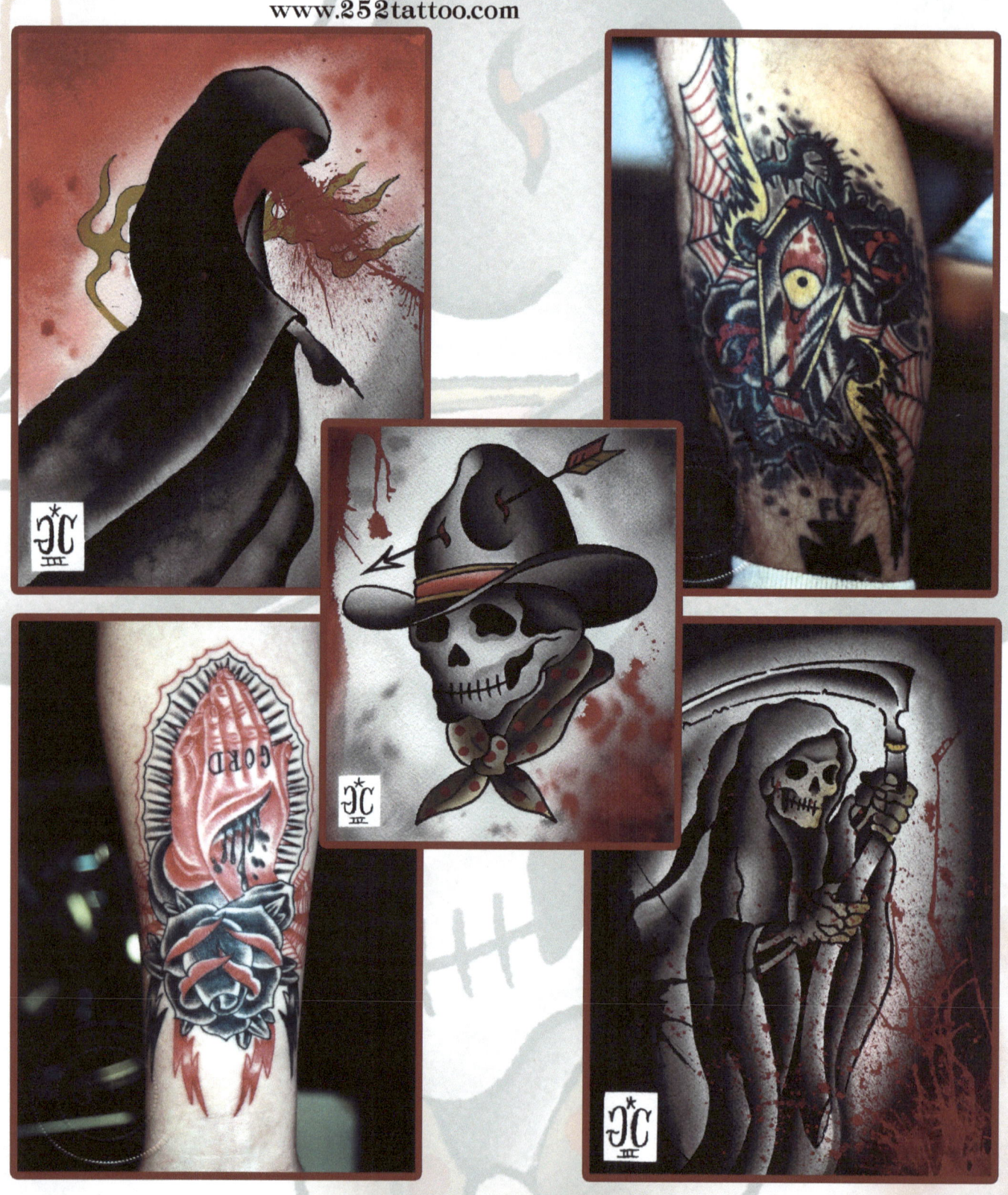

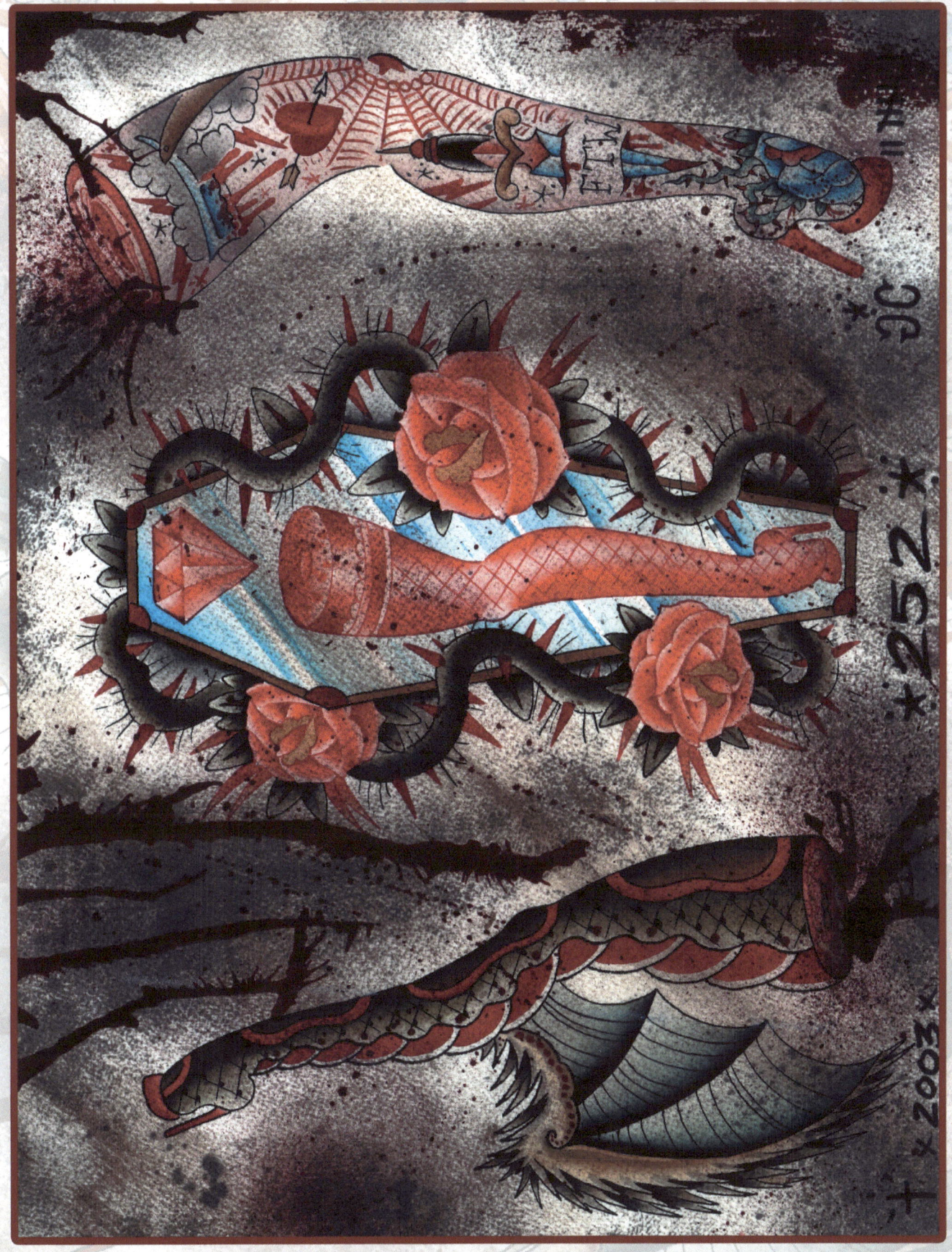

Jason Brooks

Perfection Tattoo 4205 Guadalupe Austin, TX 78751
(512) 453-2089
www.jasonbrookstattoo.com

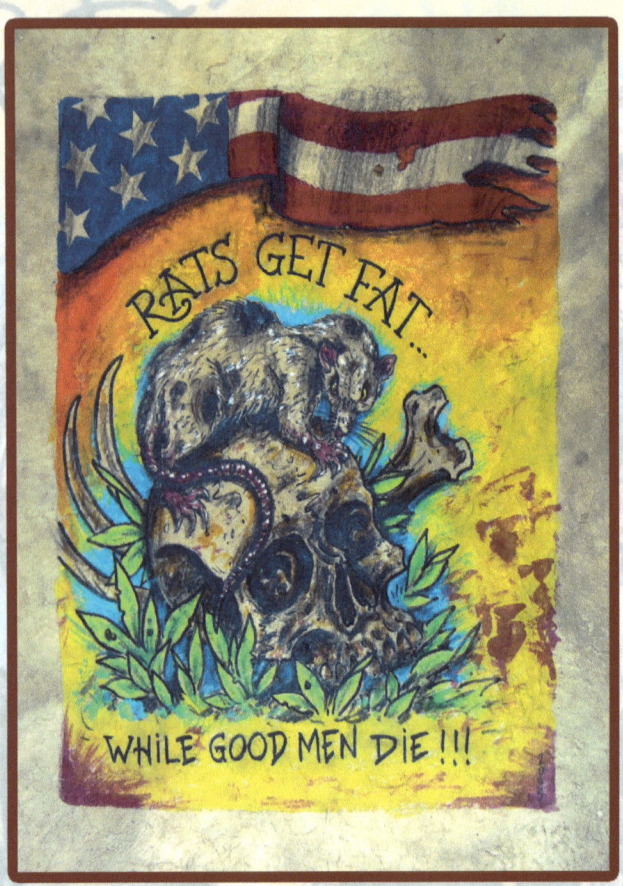

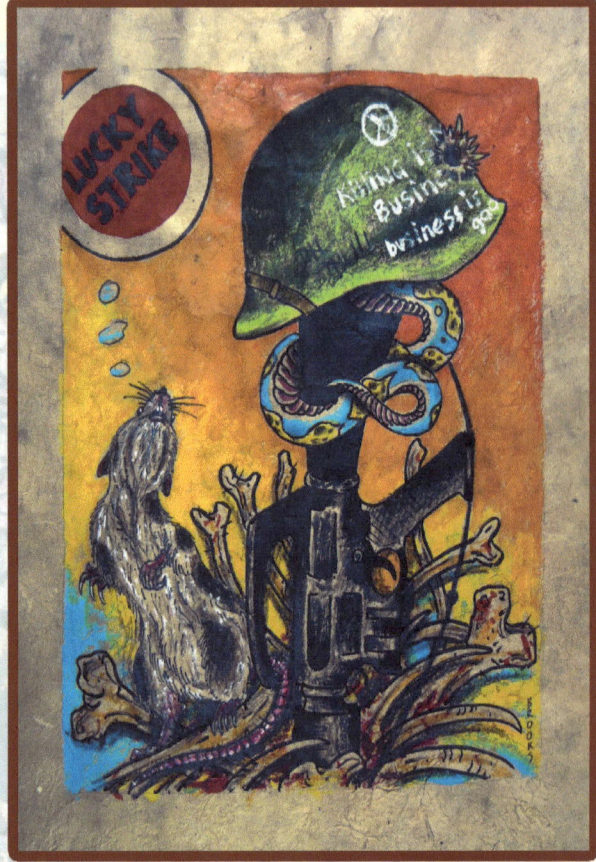

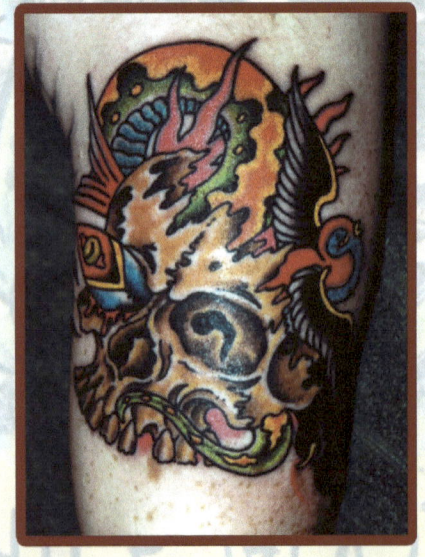

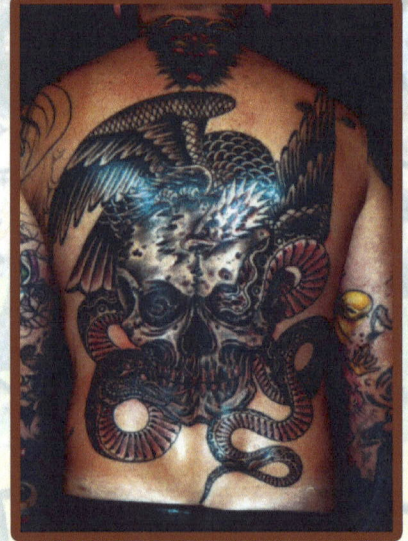

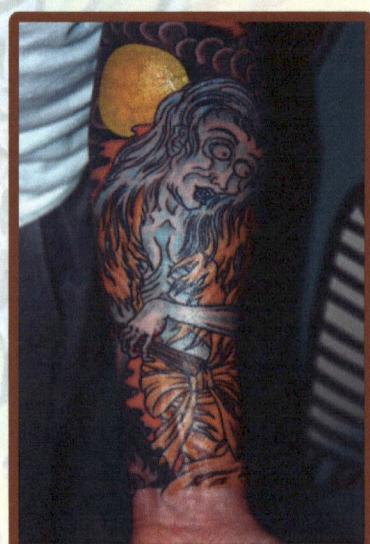

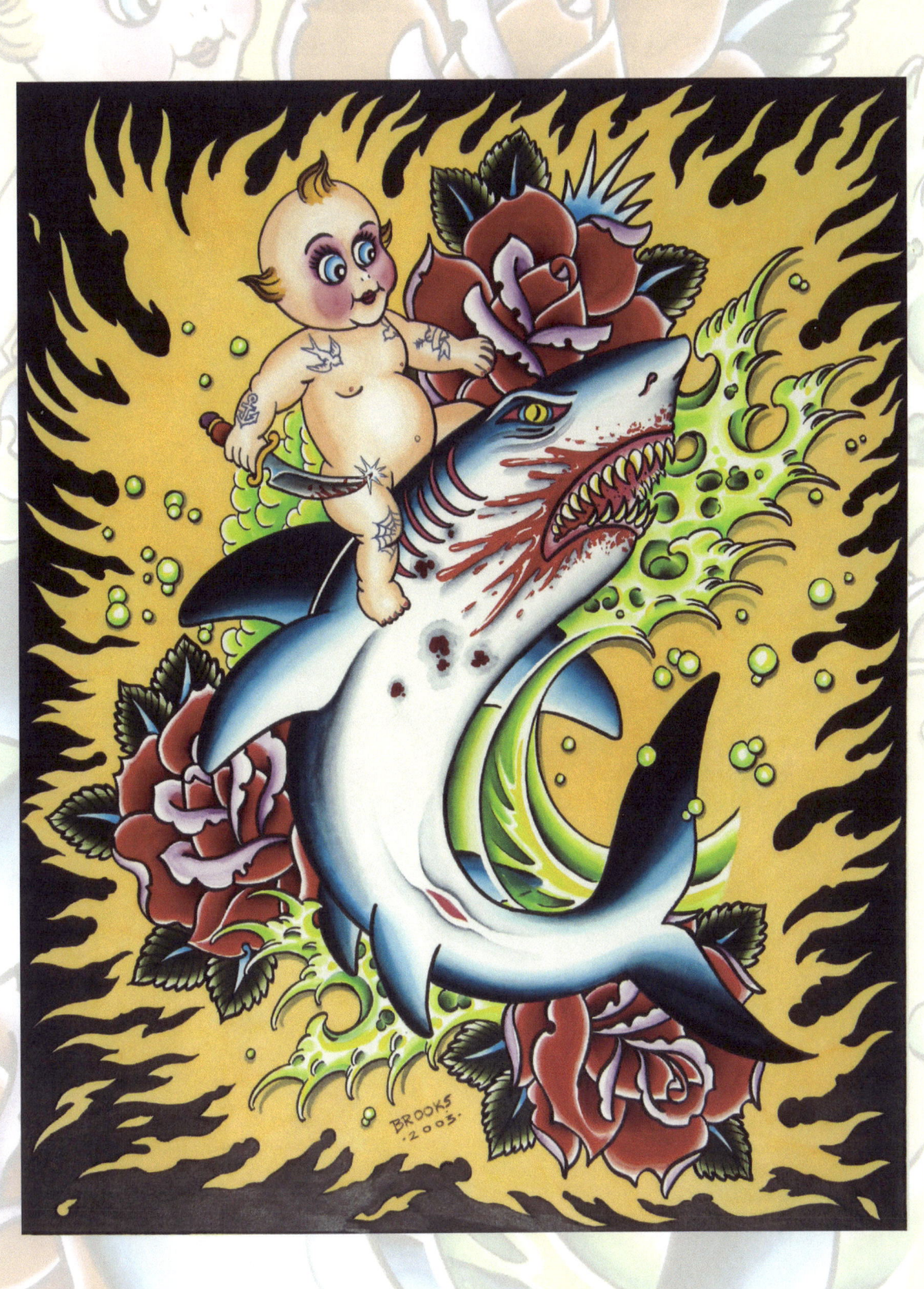

Martin Lacasse

Port City Tattoo 1305 S. College St. Wilmington, NC 28403
(910) 793-0102

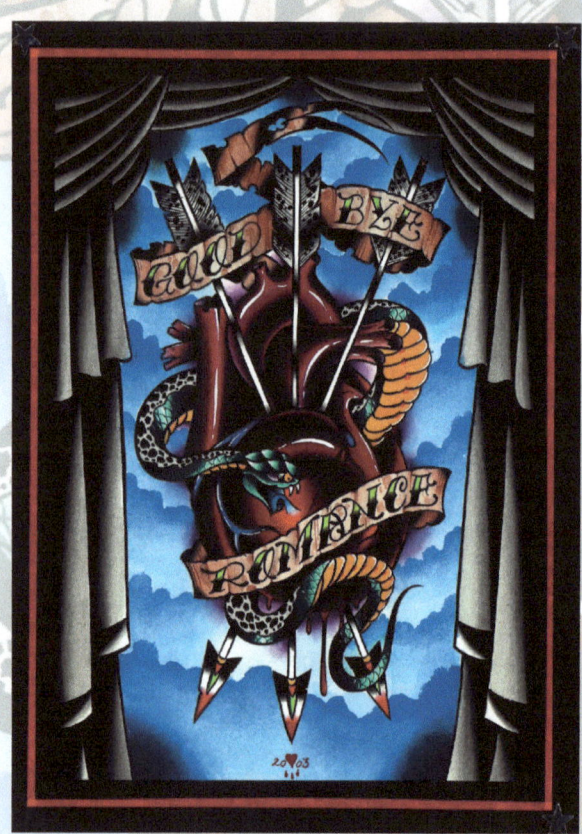

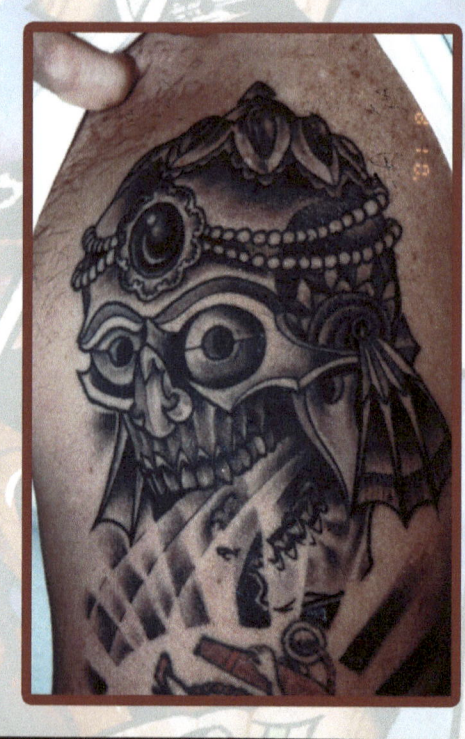

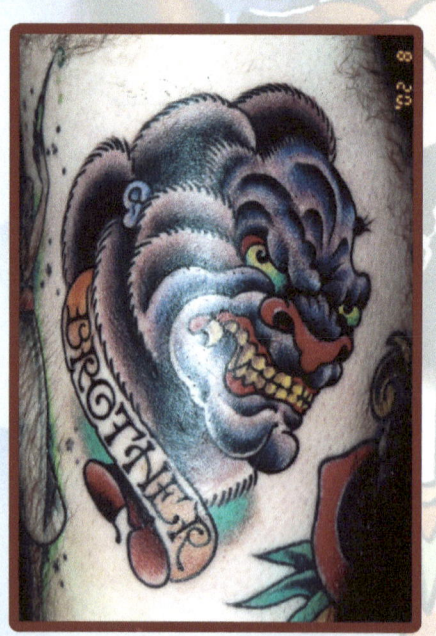

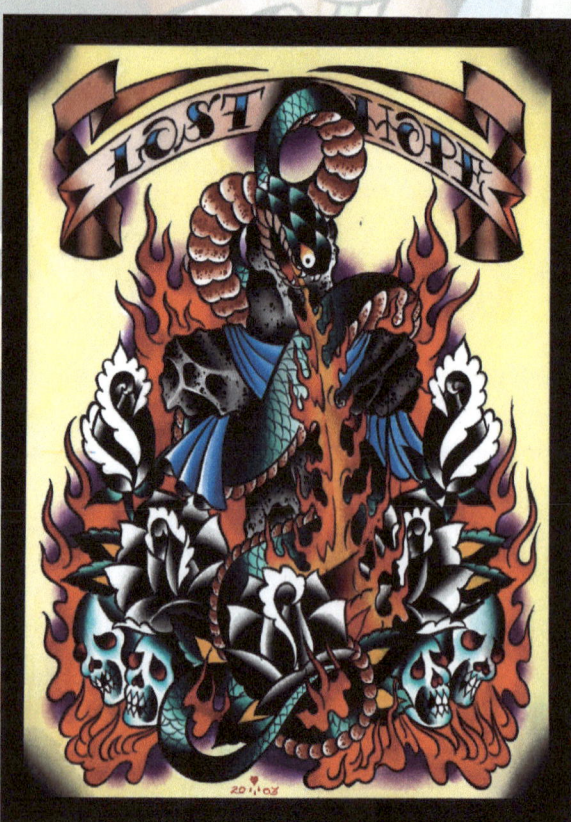

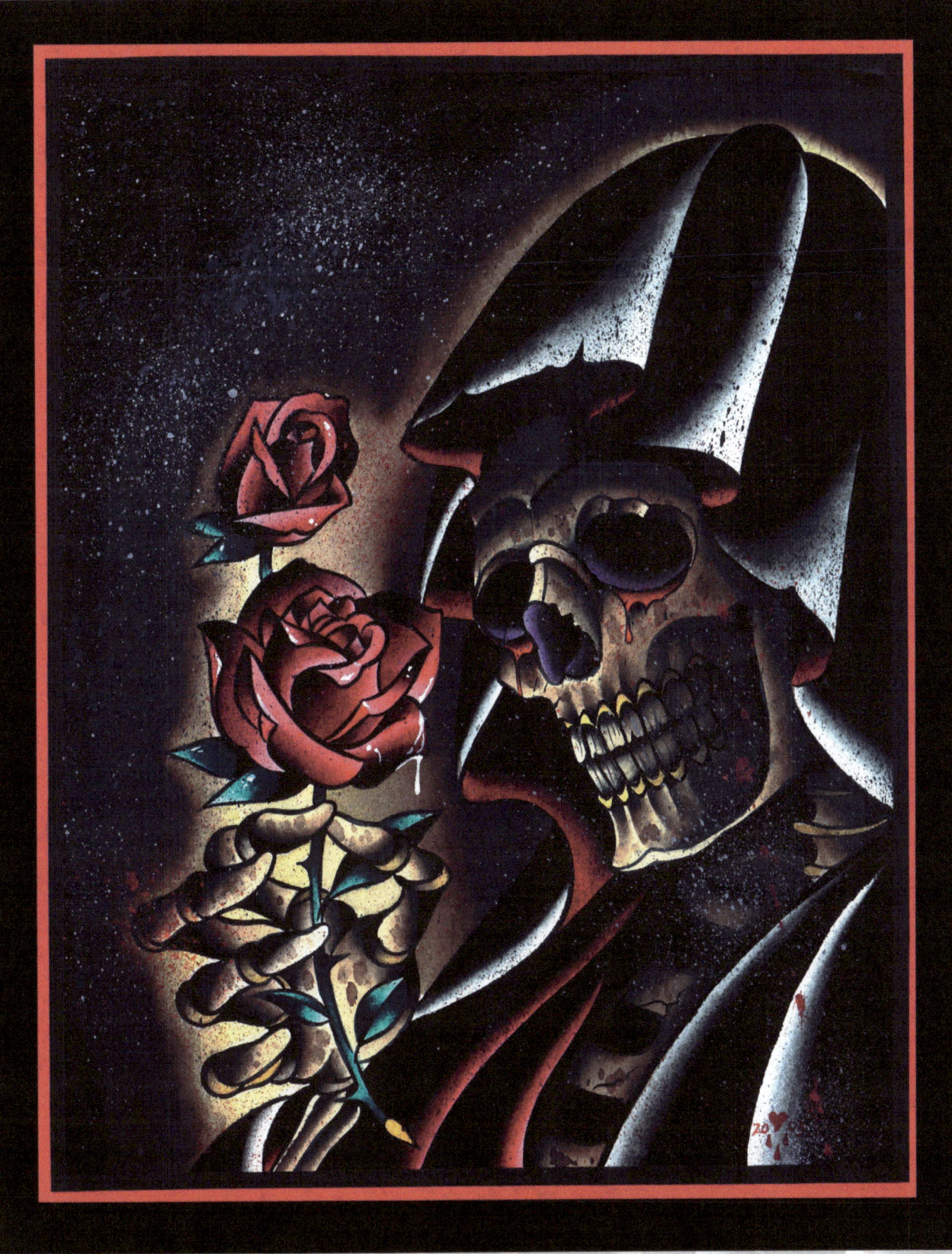

Jeff Zuck

Name Brand Tattoo 621 Church St. 2nd Floor Ann Arbor, MI 48104
(734) 623-0553

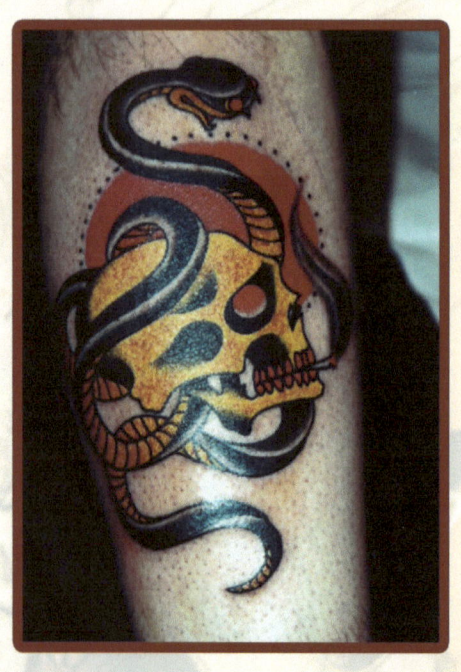

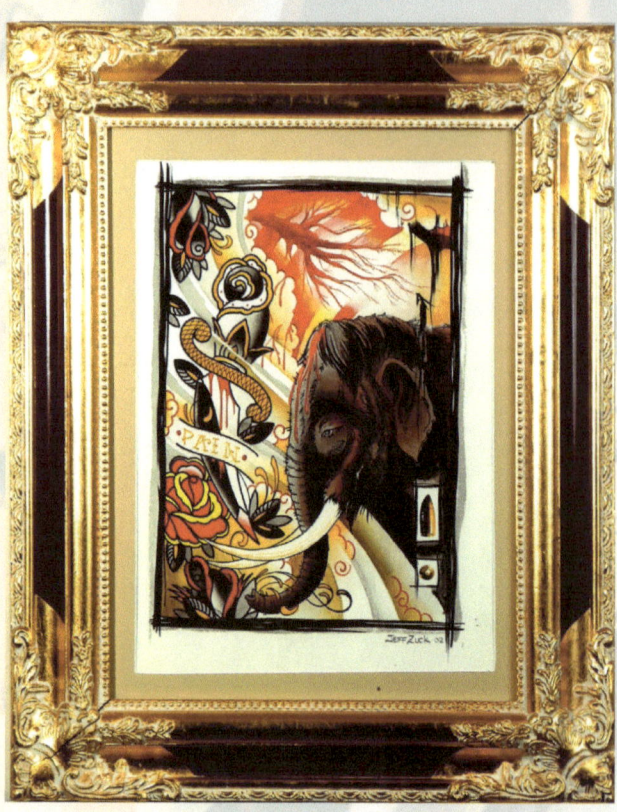

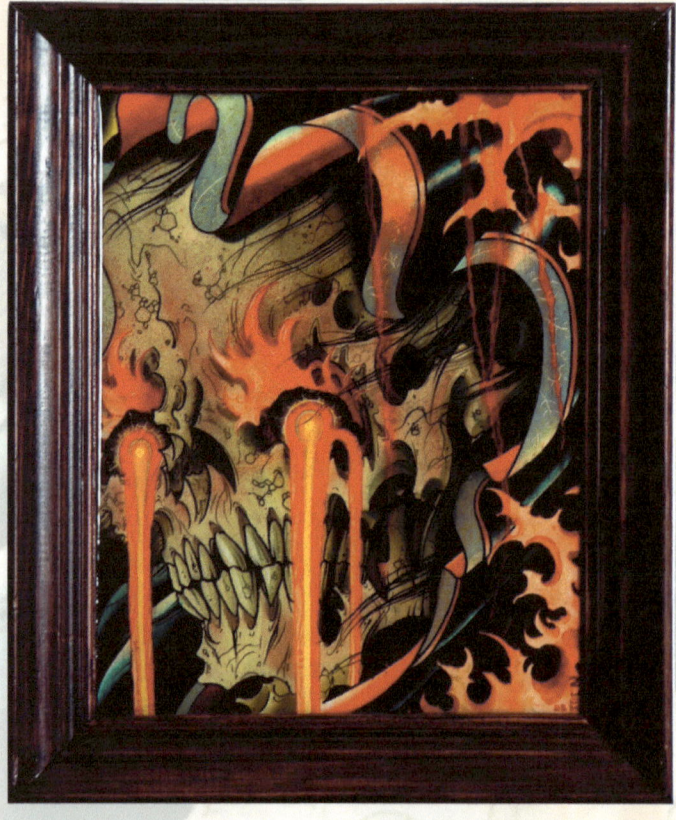

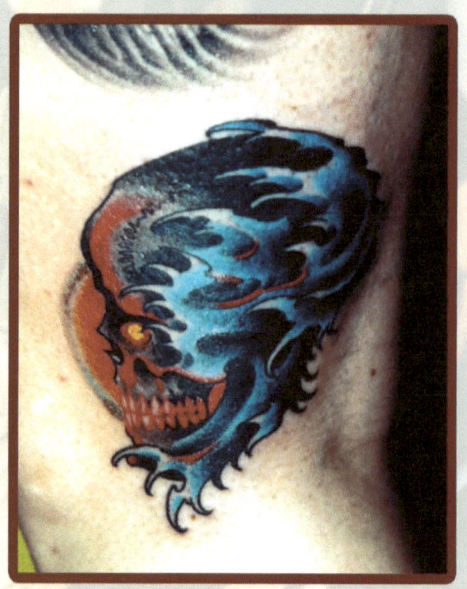

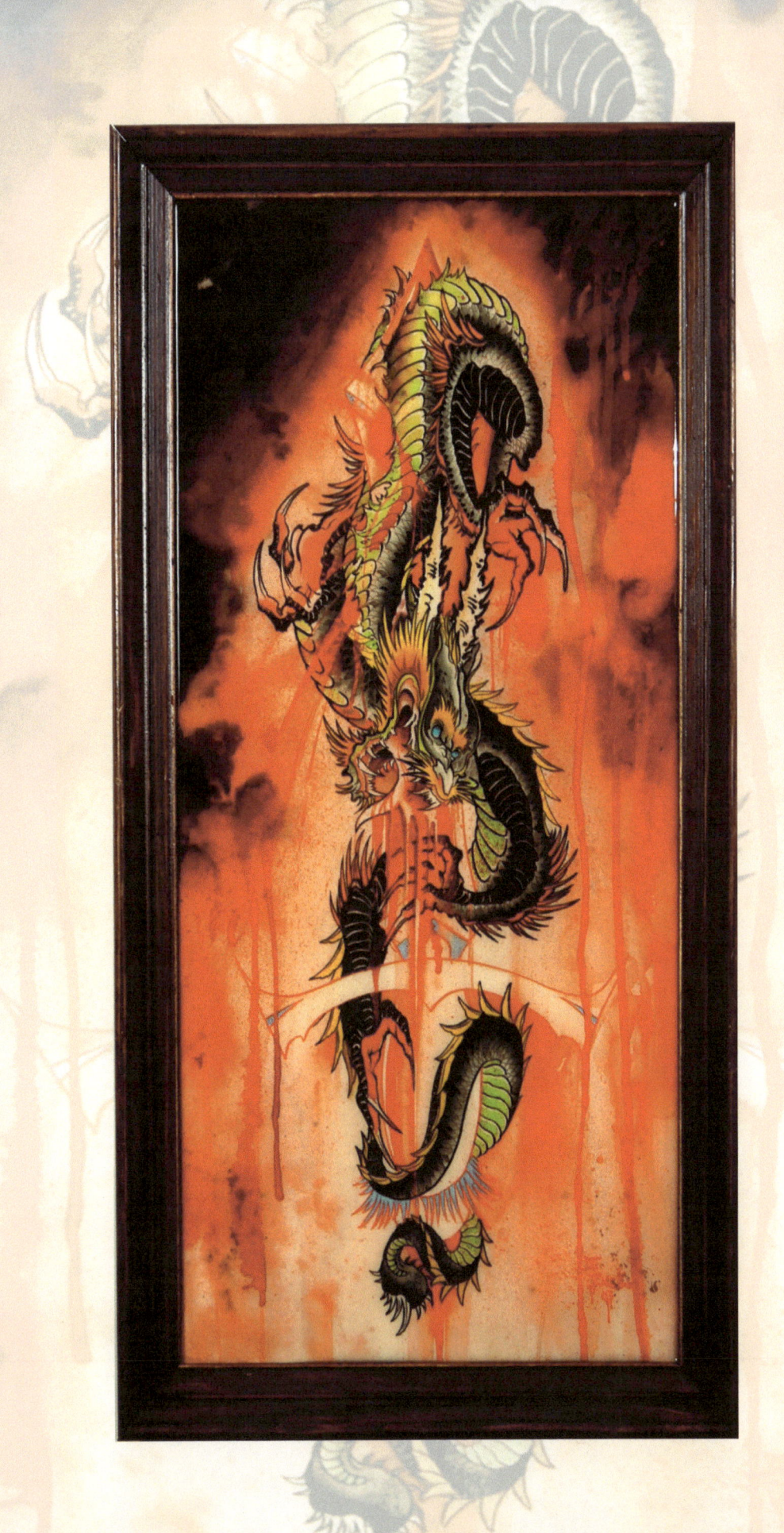

Bryan Randolph

Everlasting Tattoo 813 Divisadero St. San Francisco, CA 94117
(415) 928-6244
www.everlastingtattoo.com

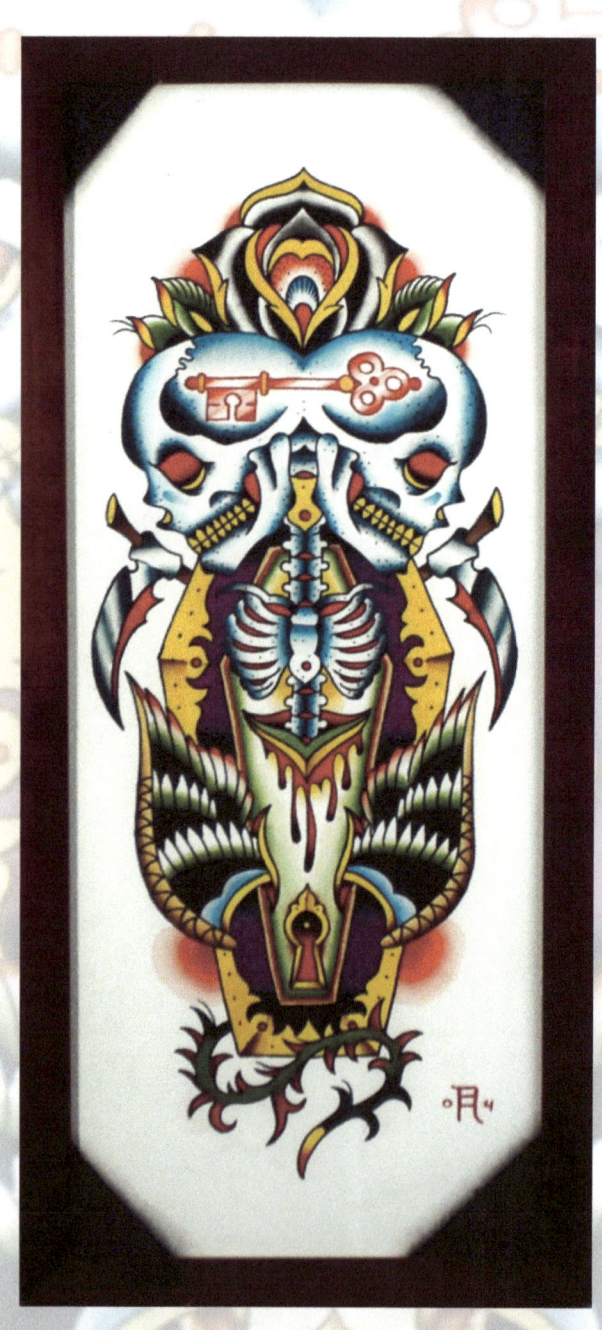

Jef Wright

Magnum Tattooing Inc
2317 Division Avenue South, Grand Rapids, MI 49507
(616) 245-1880

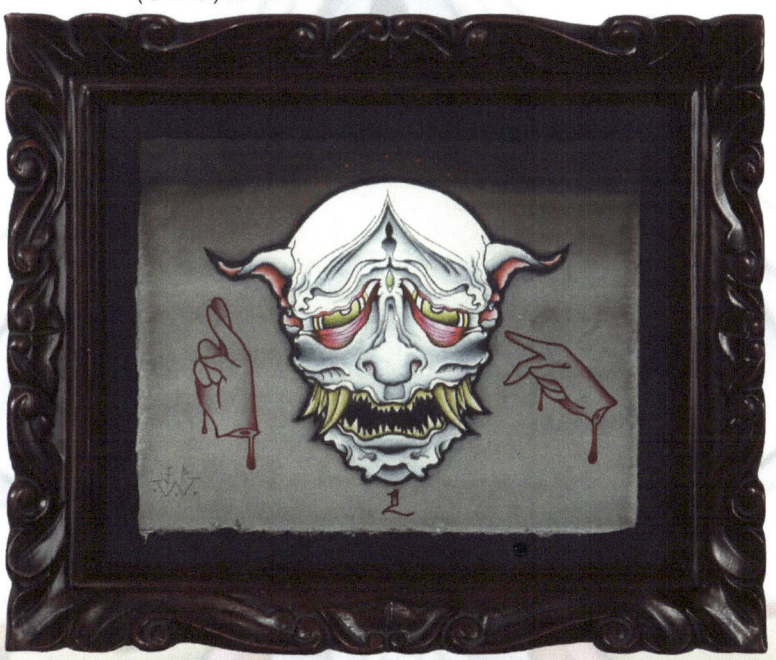

Eric Thrice

Tattoo Circus
8835 Southwest 40th Street, Miami, FL 33165
(305) 207-6522

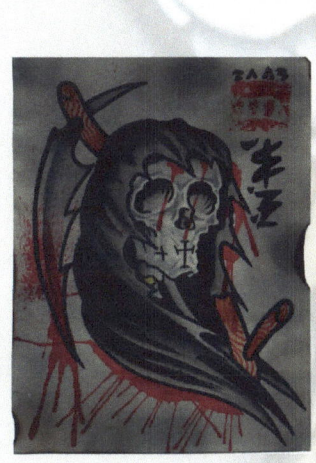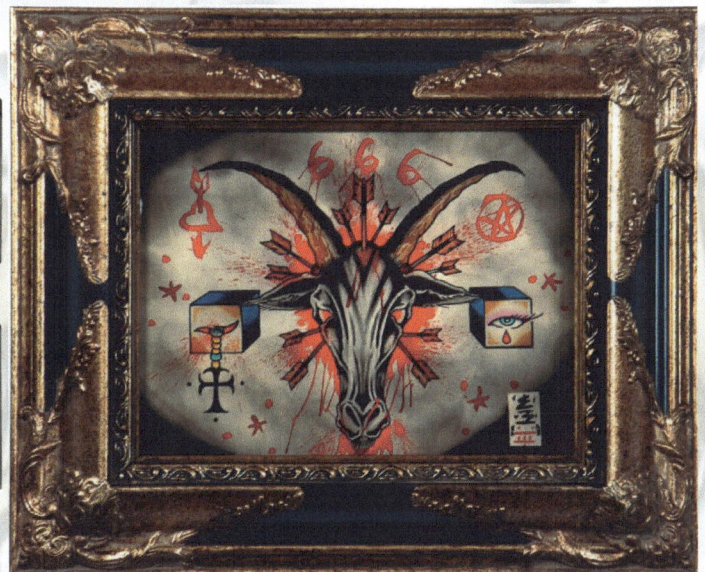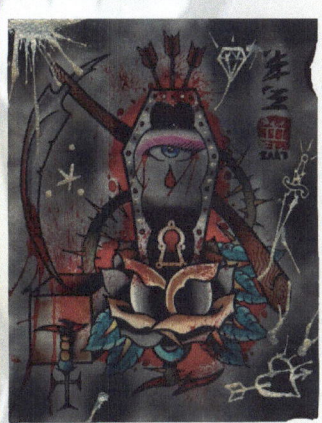

Dave Fox

Olde City Tattoo 44 S. 2nd Street Philadelphia, PA 19106
(215)627-6271
www.evilballs.com

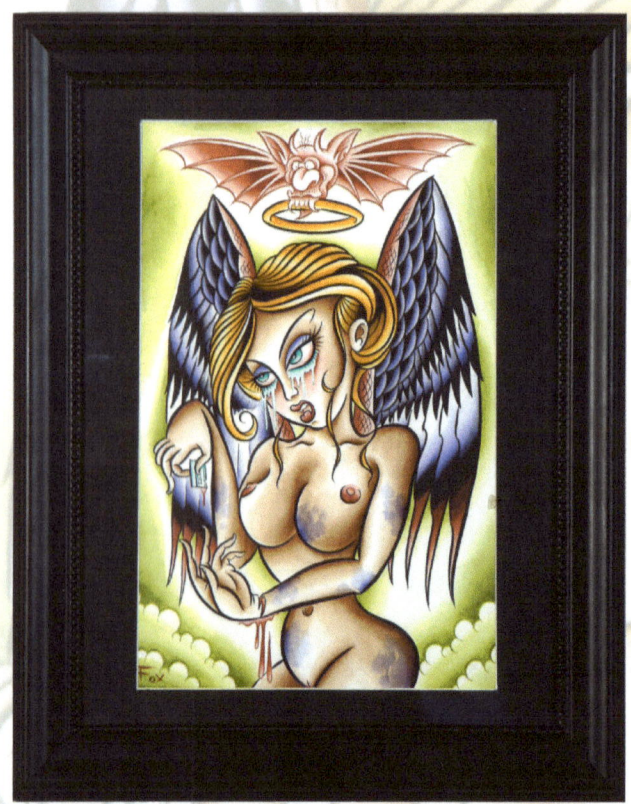

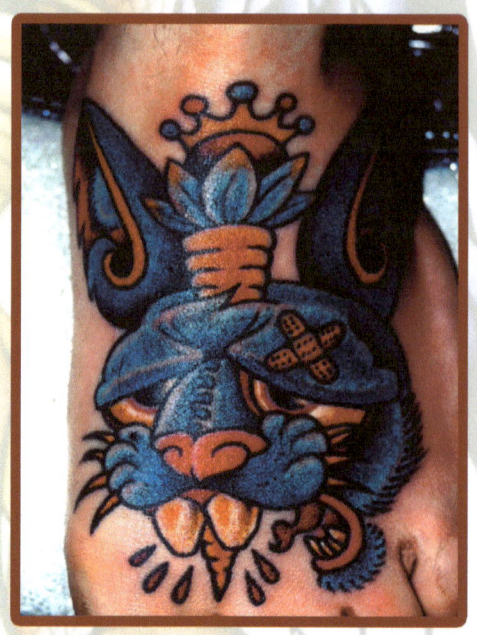

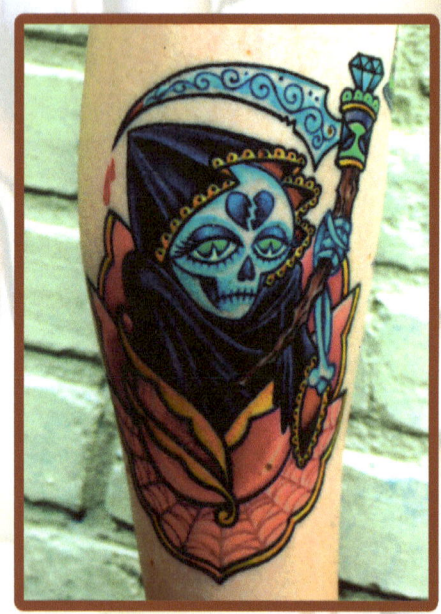

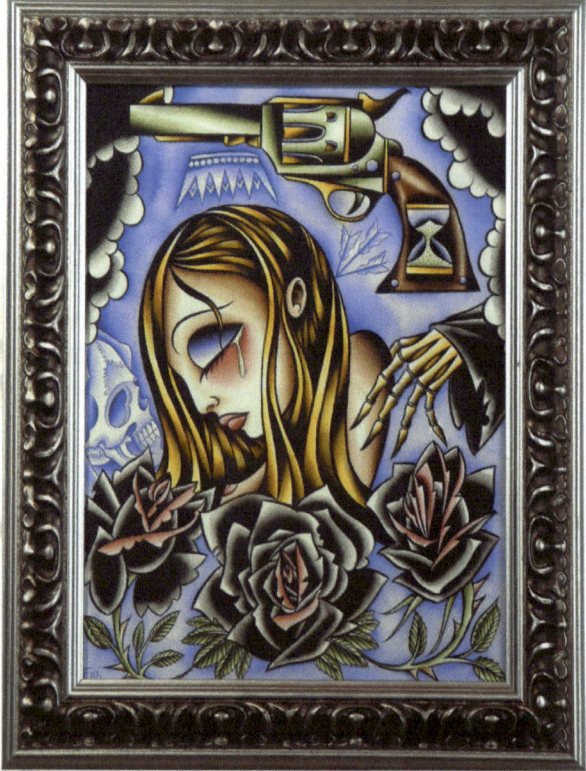

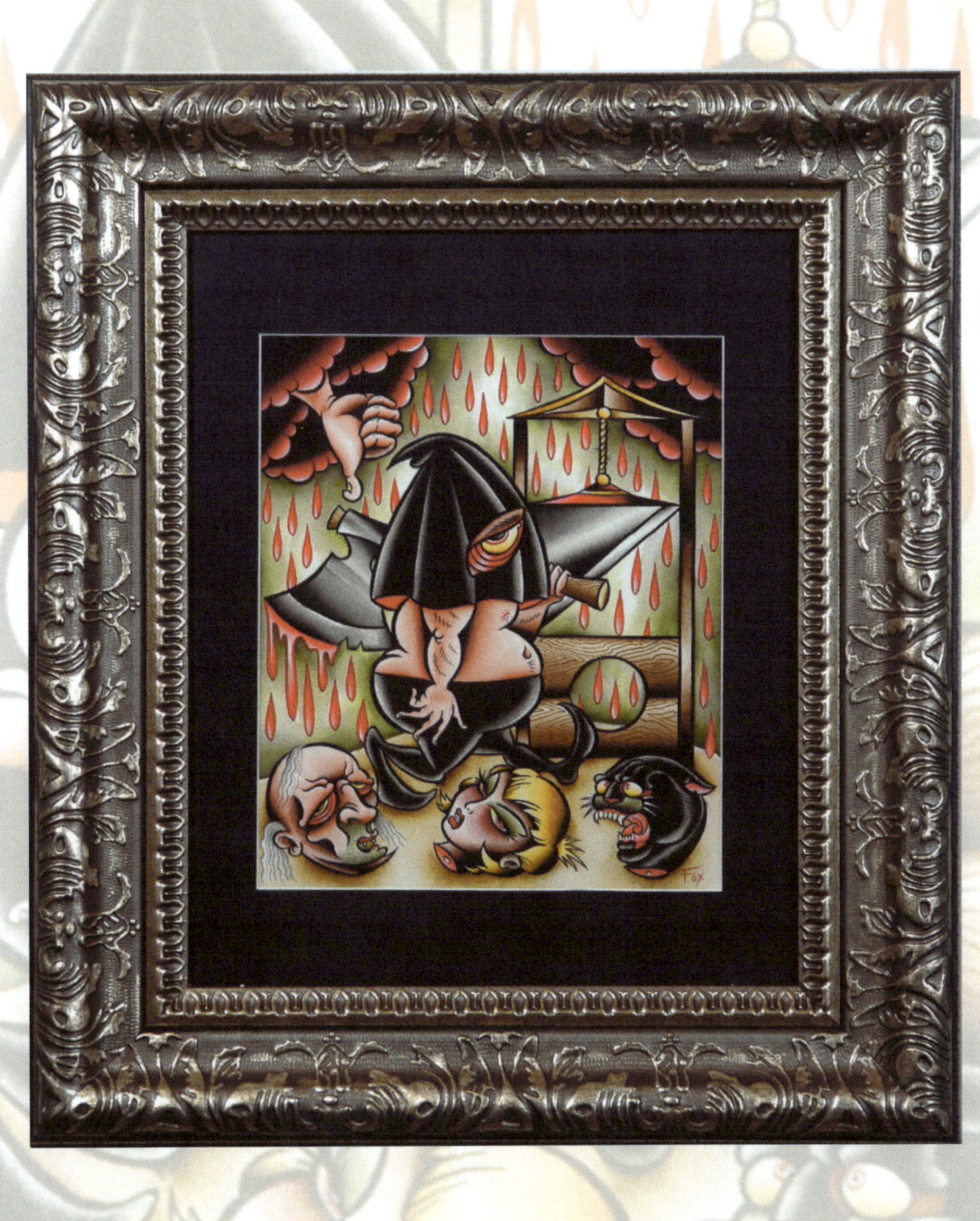

Mario Desa

Deluxe Tattoo 1459 W. Irving Chicago, Il 19106
(773) 549-1594
www.deluxetattoo.com

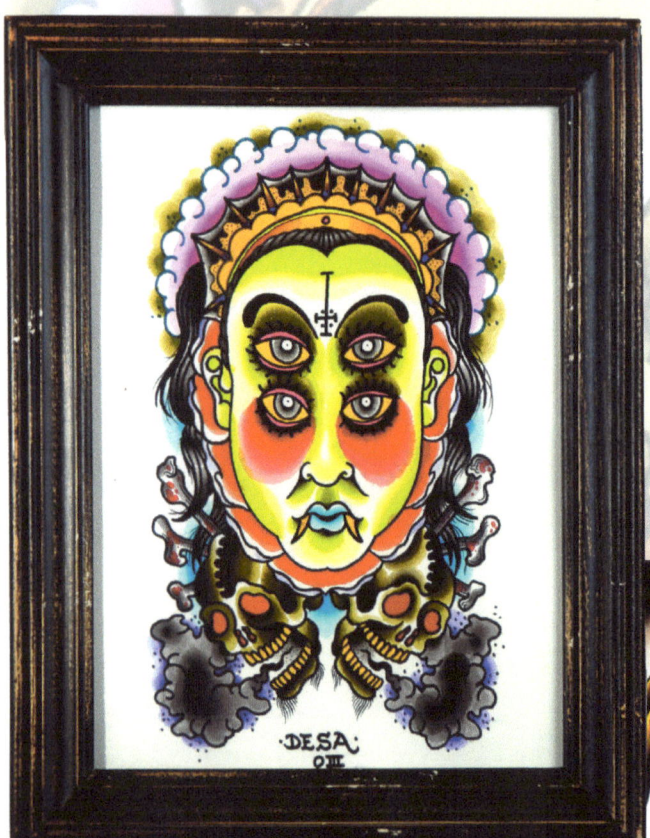

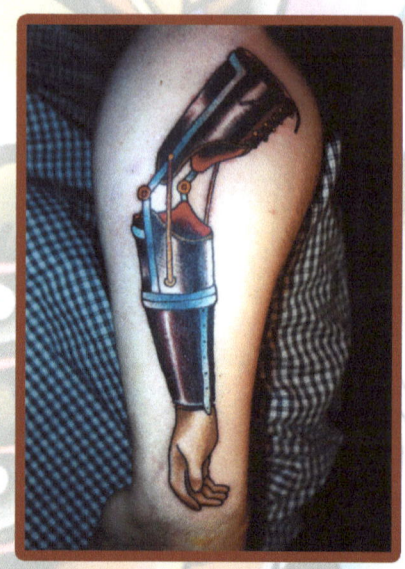

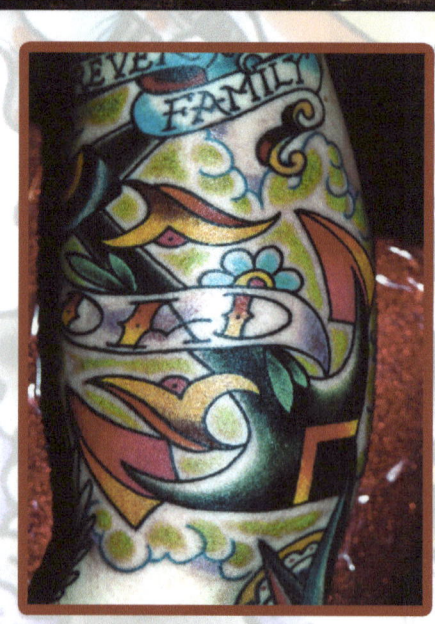

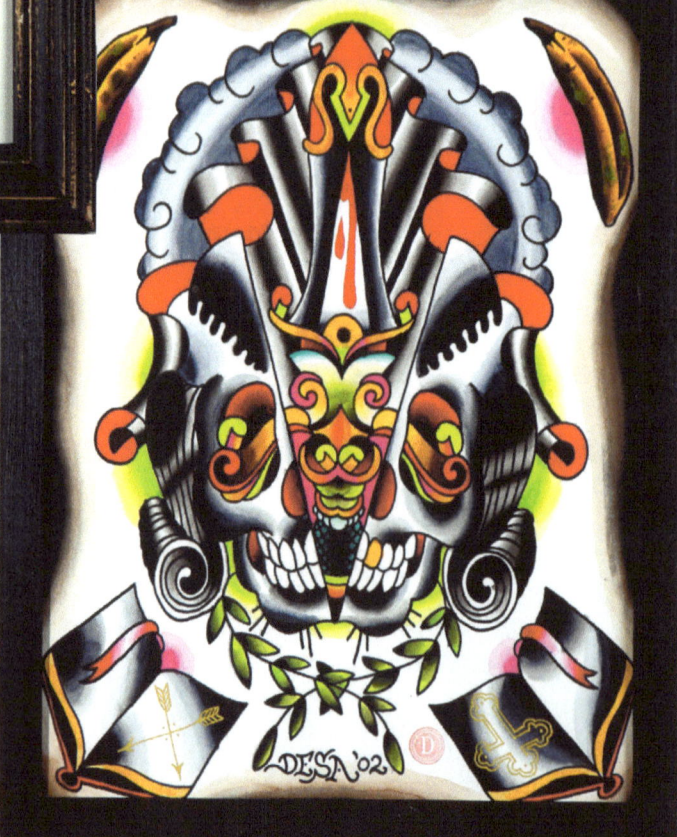

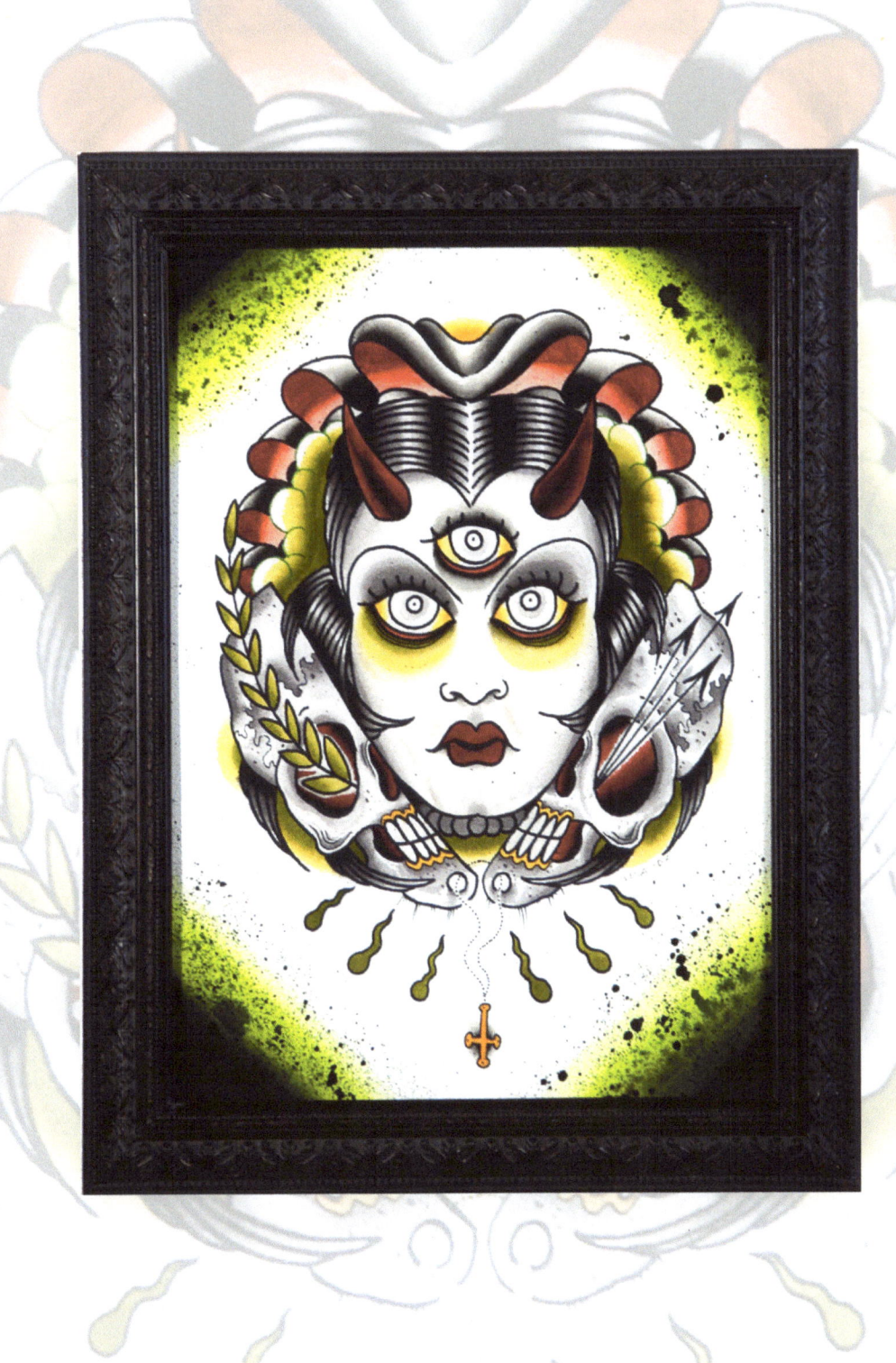

Chris Trevino

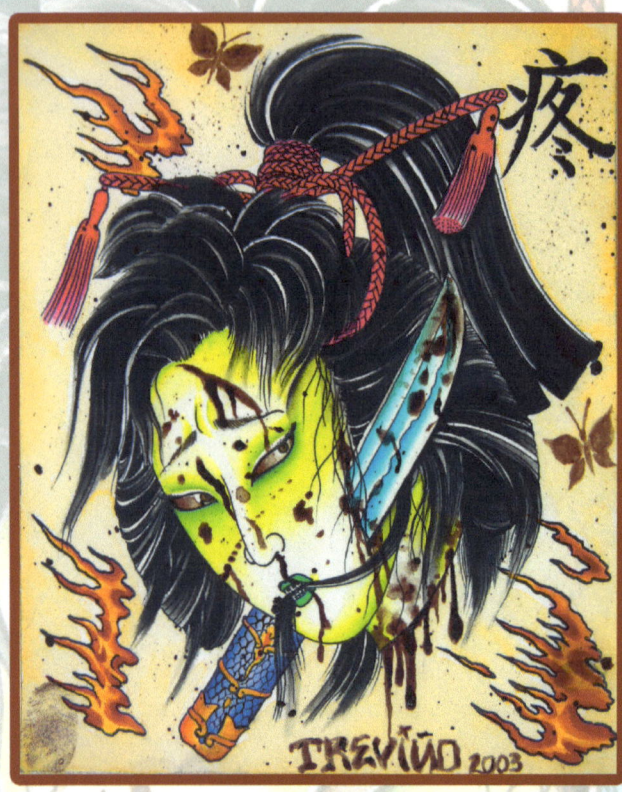

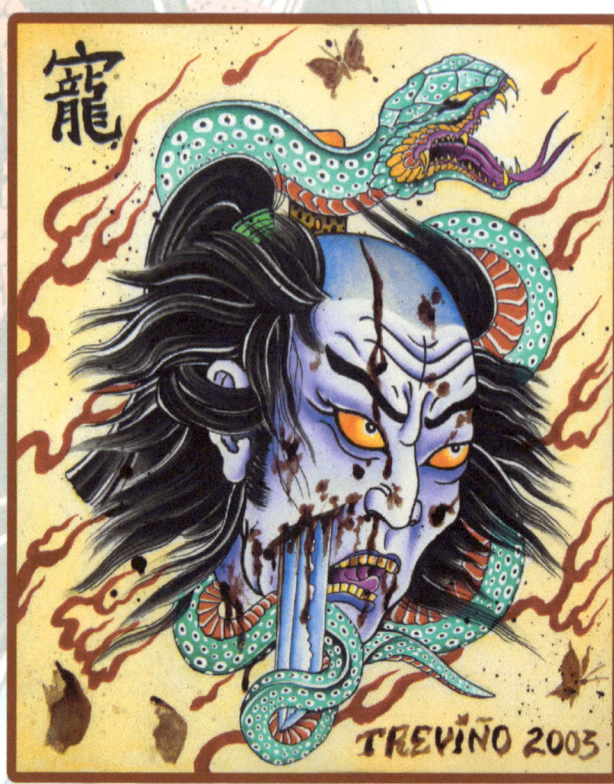

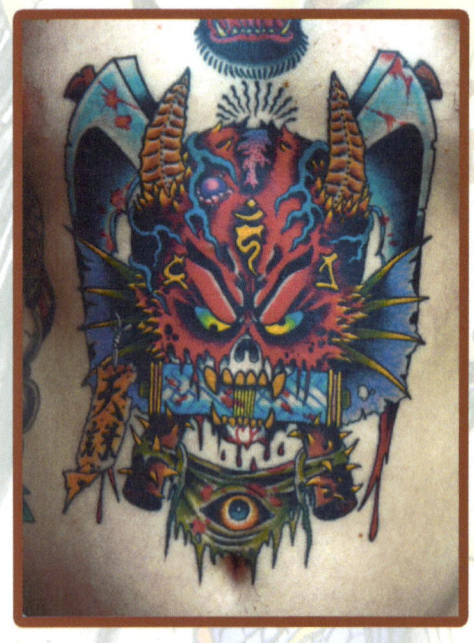

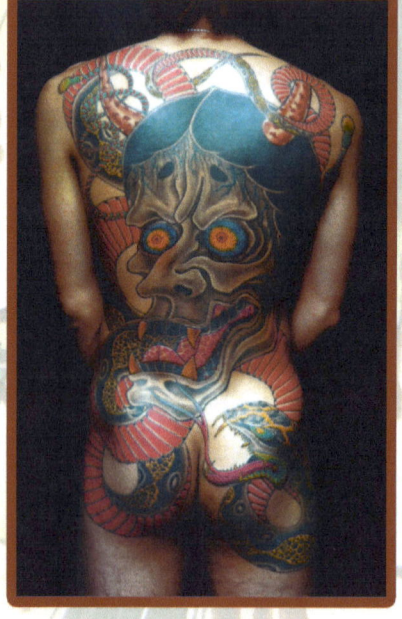

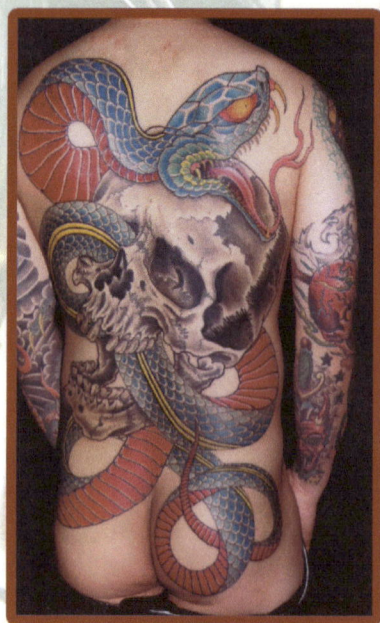

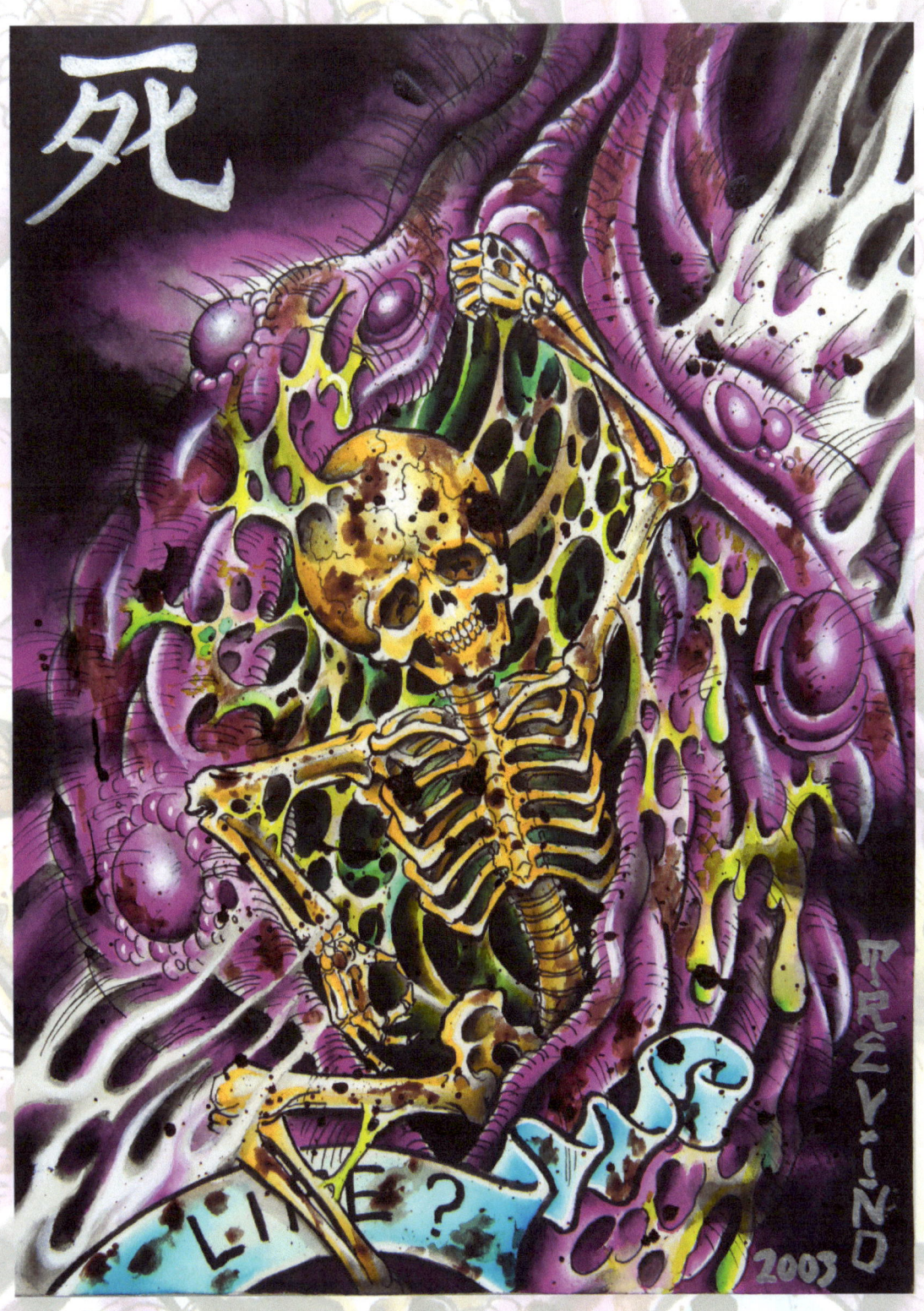

Aaron Coleman

Immaculate Tattoo 1454 W. Main St. #1 Mesa, AZ 85201
(480) 668-4940
www.immaculatetattoo.com

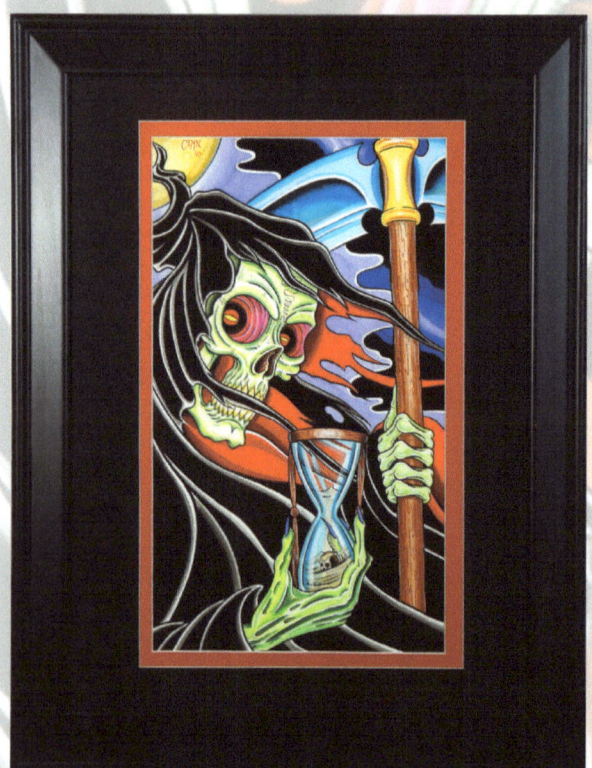

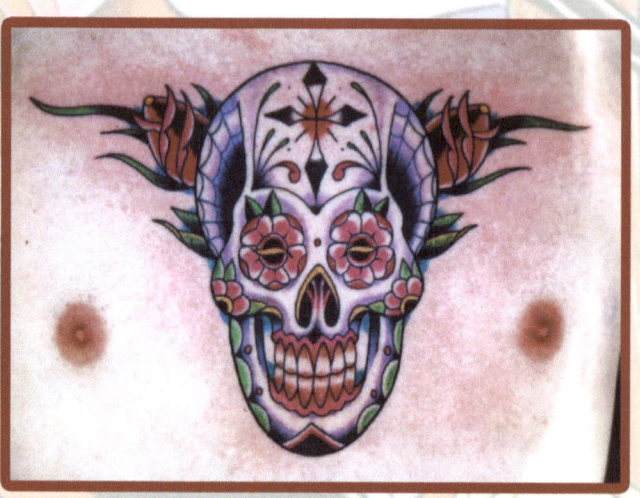

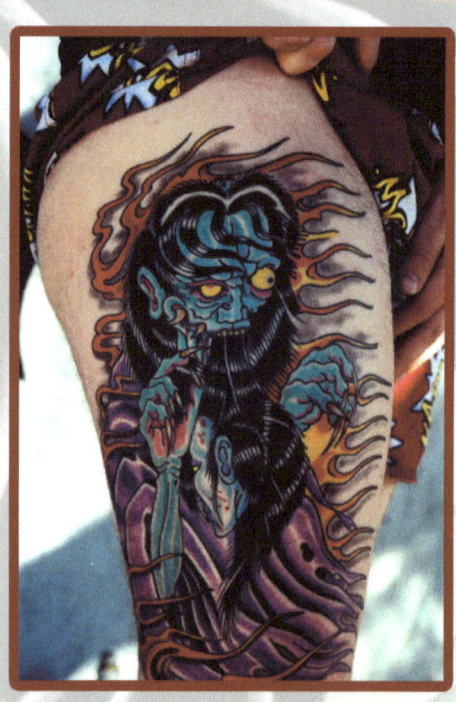

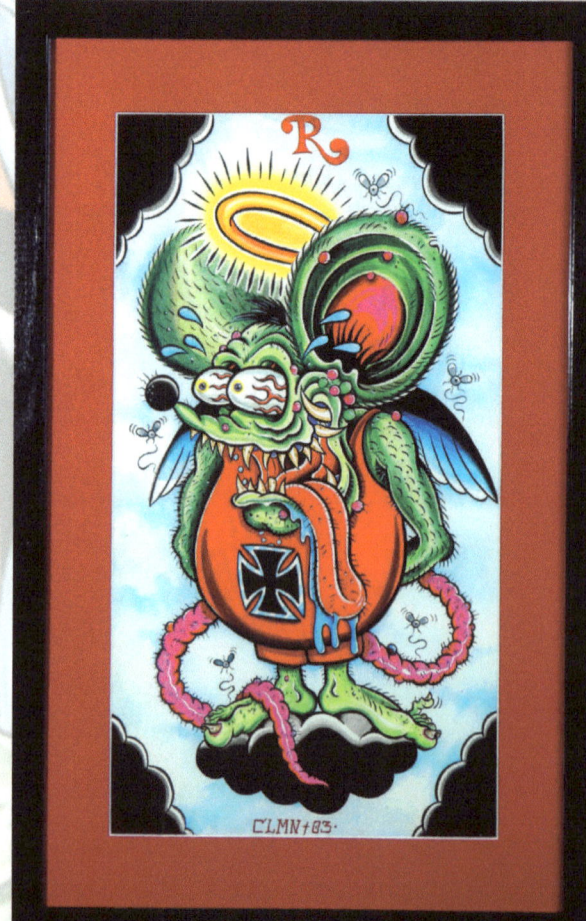

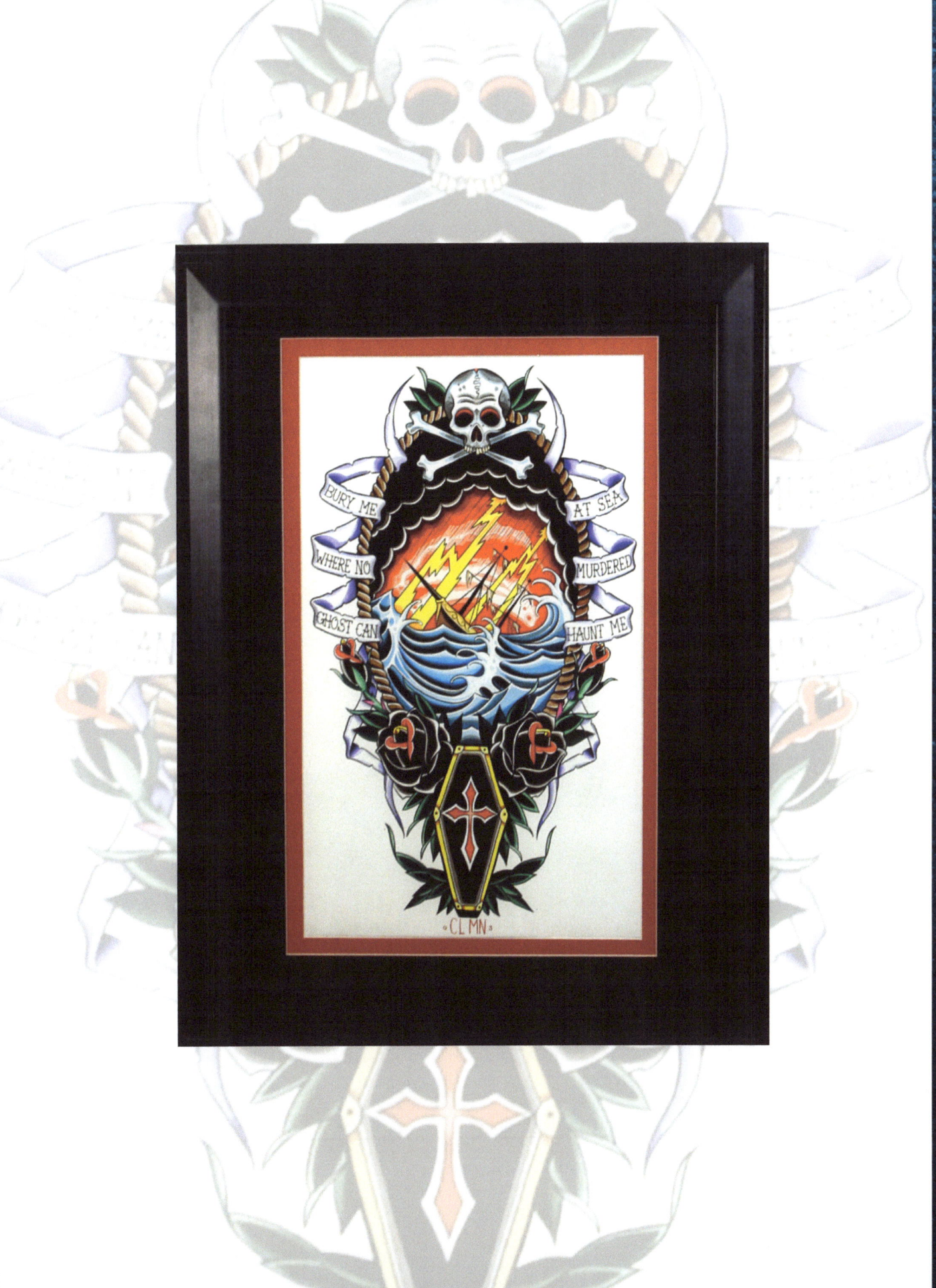

Casey Cokrlic

Pair O' Dice Tattoo 2811 Main St. Dallas, TX
(214) 741-DICE

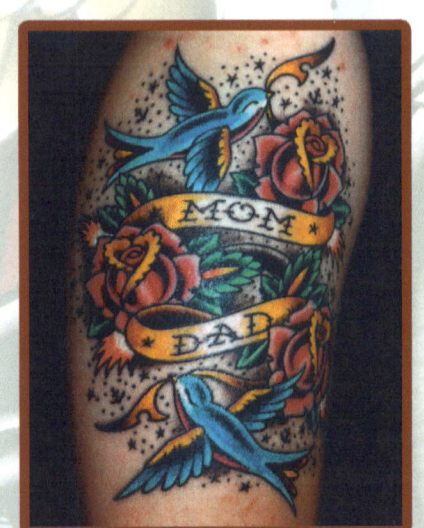

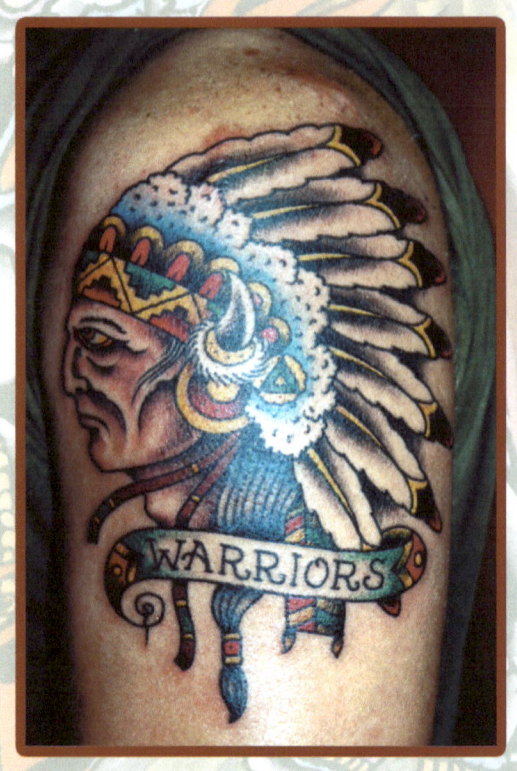

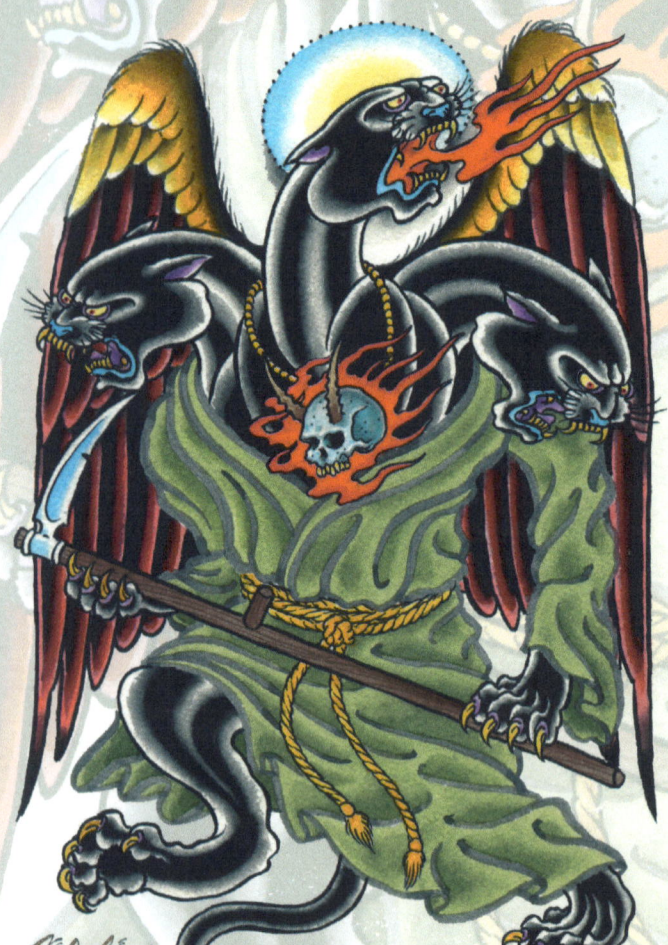

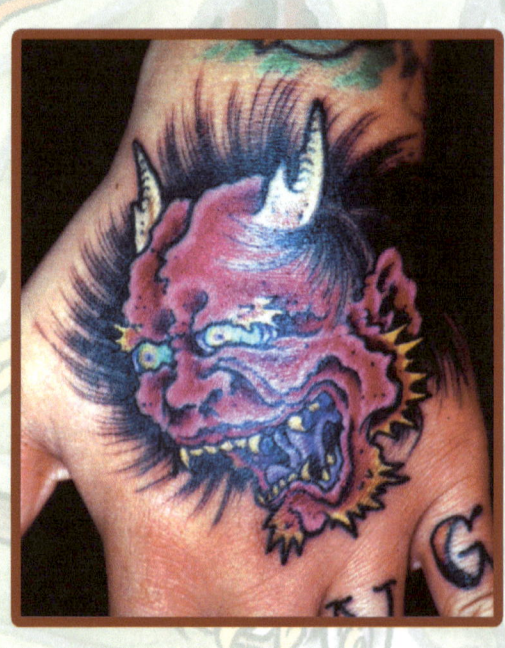

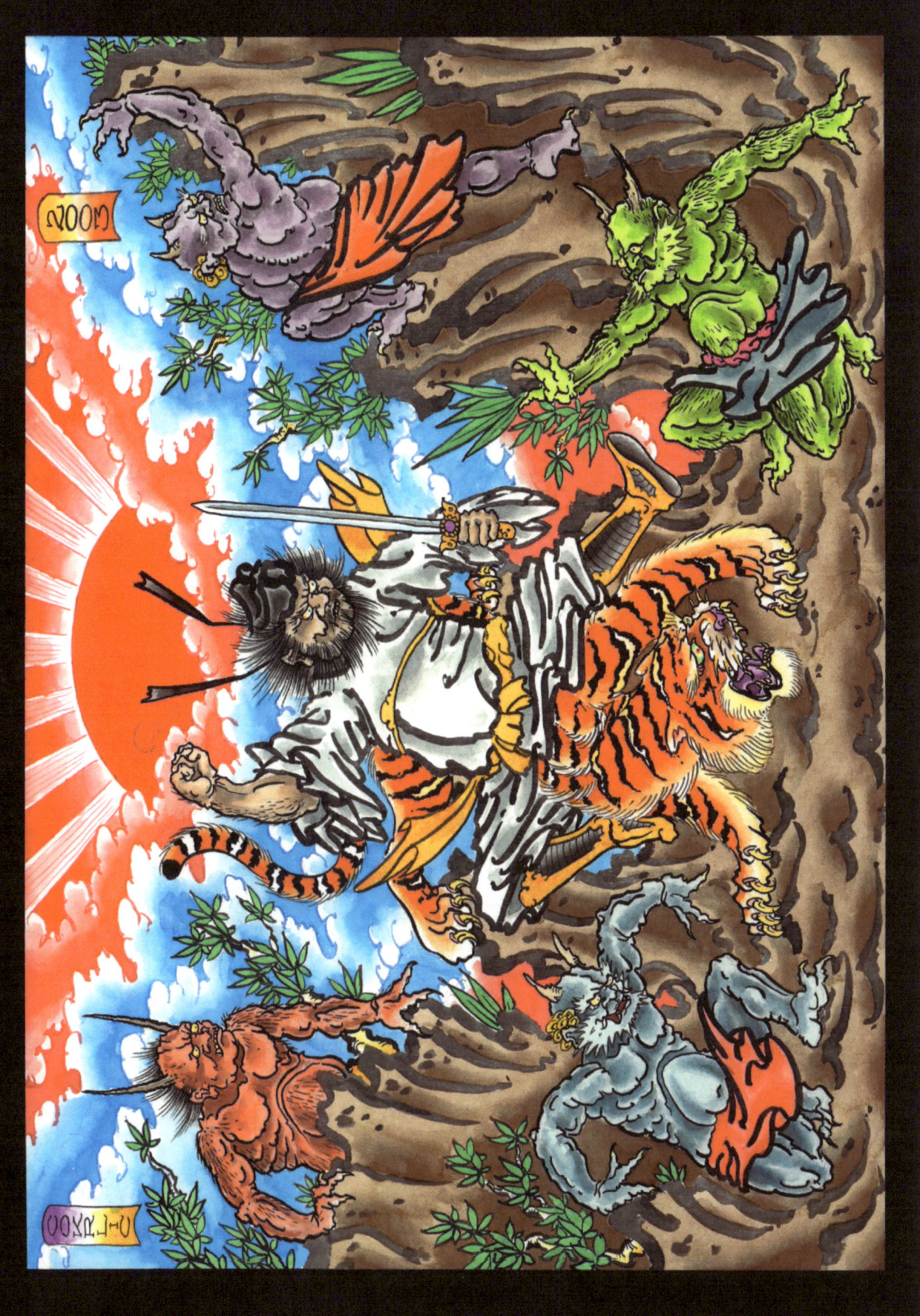

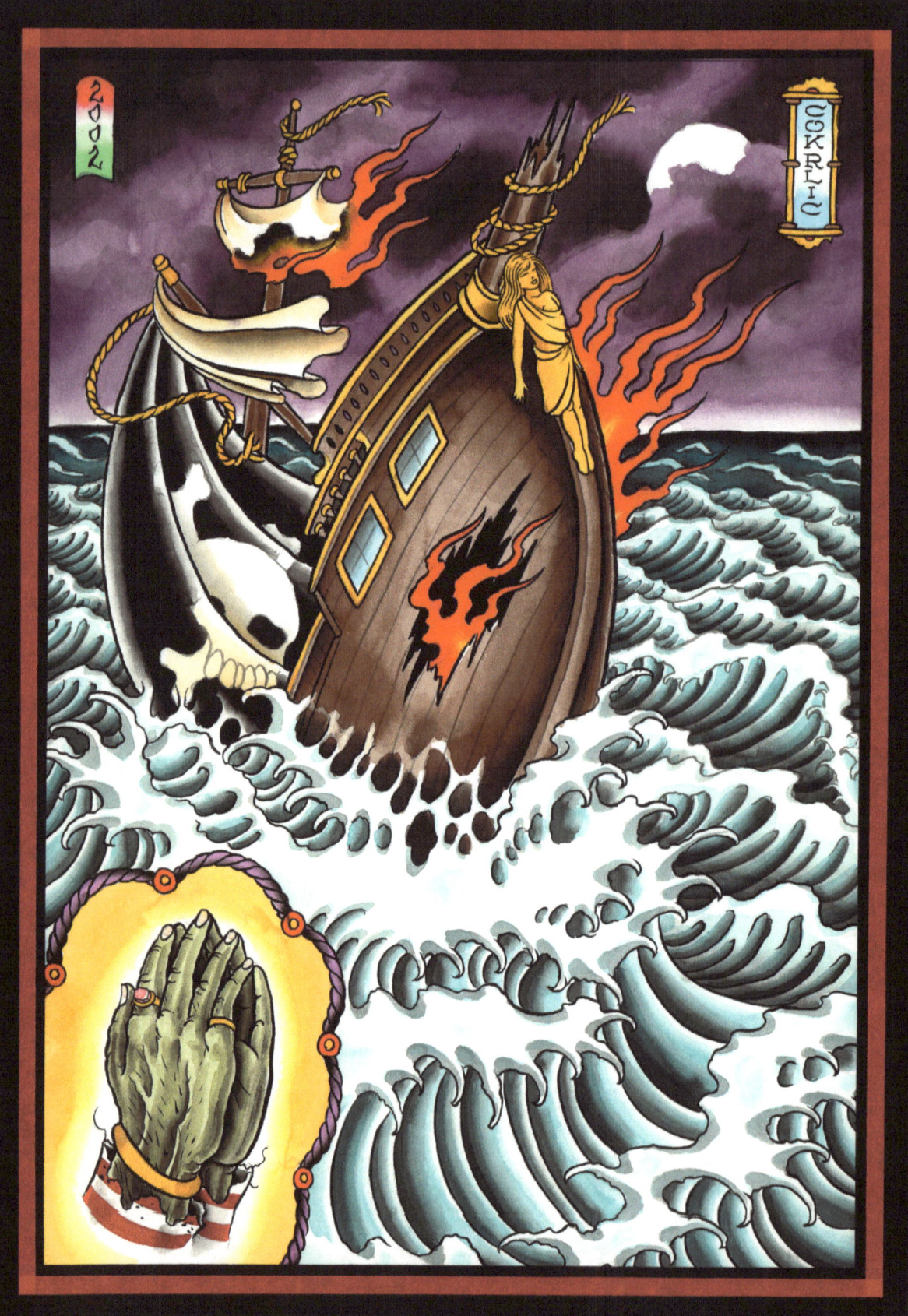

Hudge

F.U. Tattoo 1355 Capitola Rd. Santa Cruz, CA 95062
(831) 464-1669

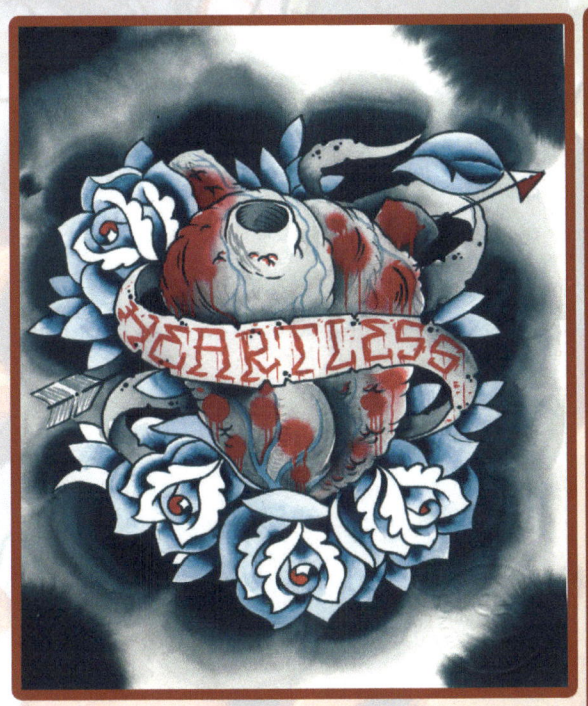

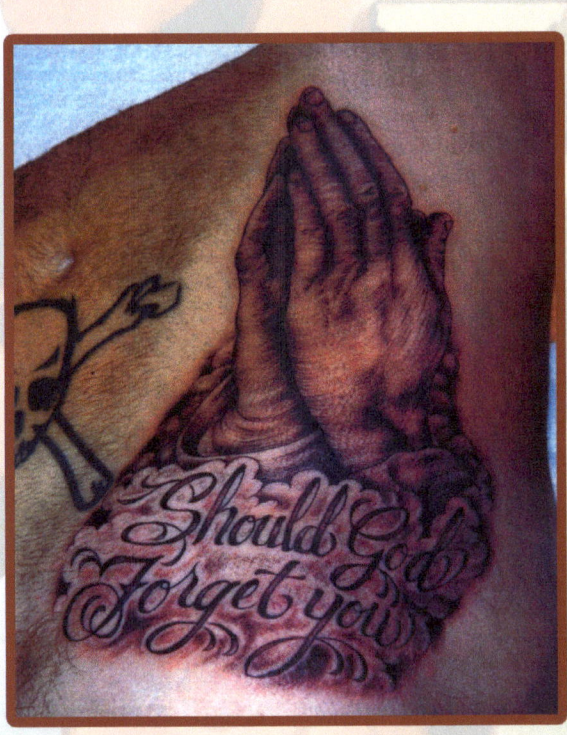

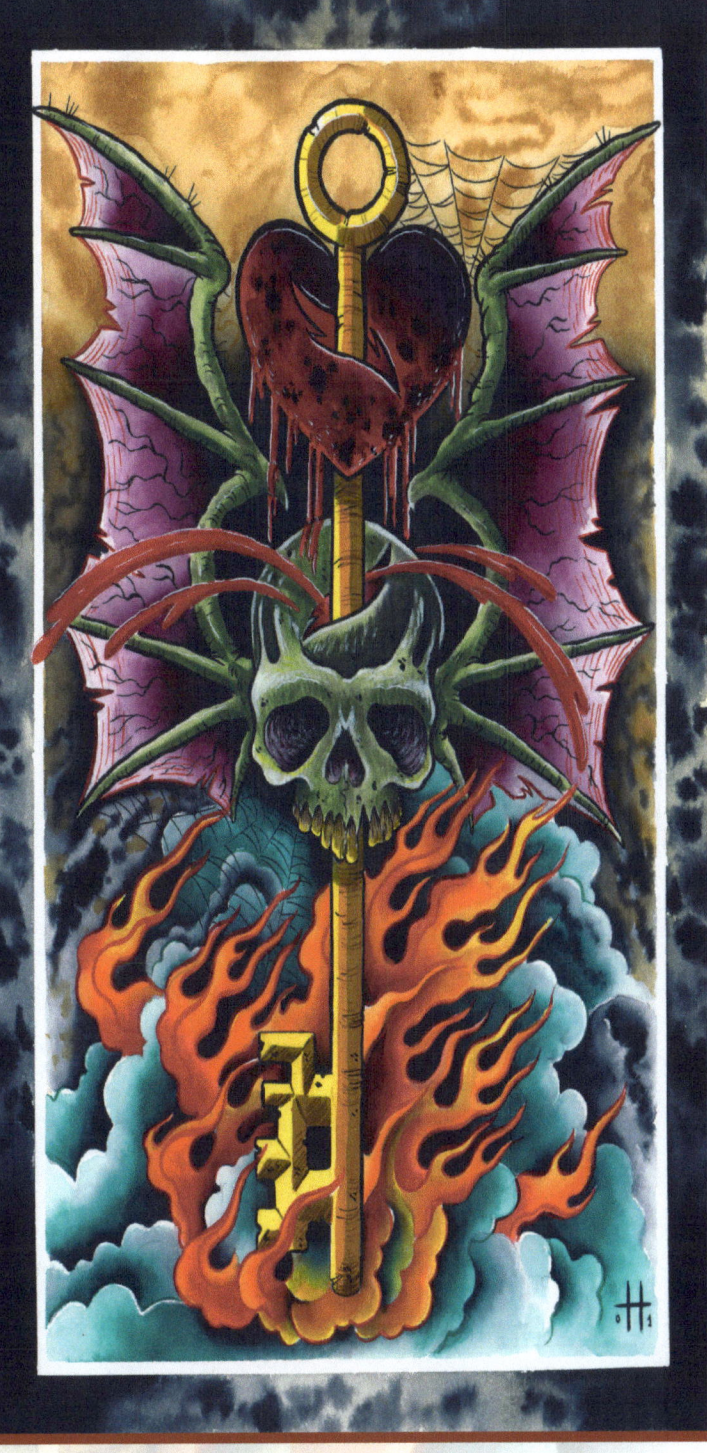

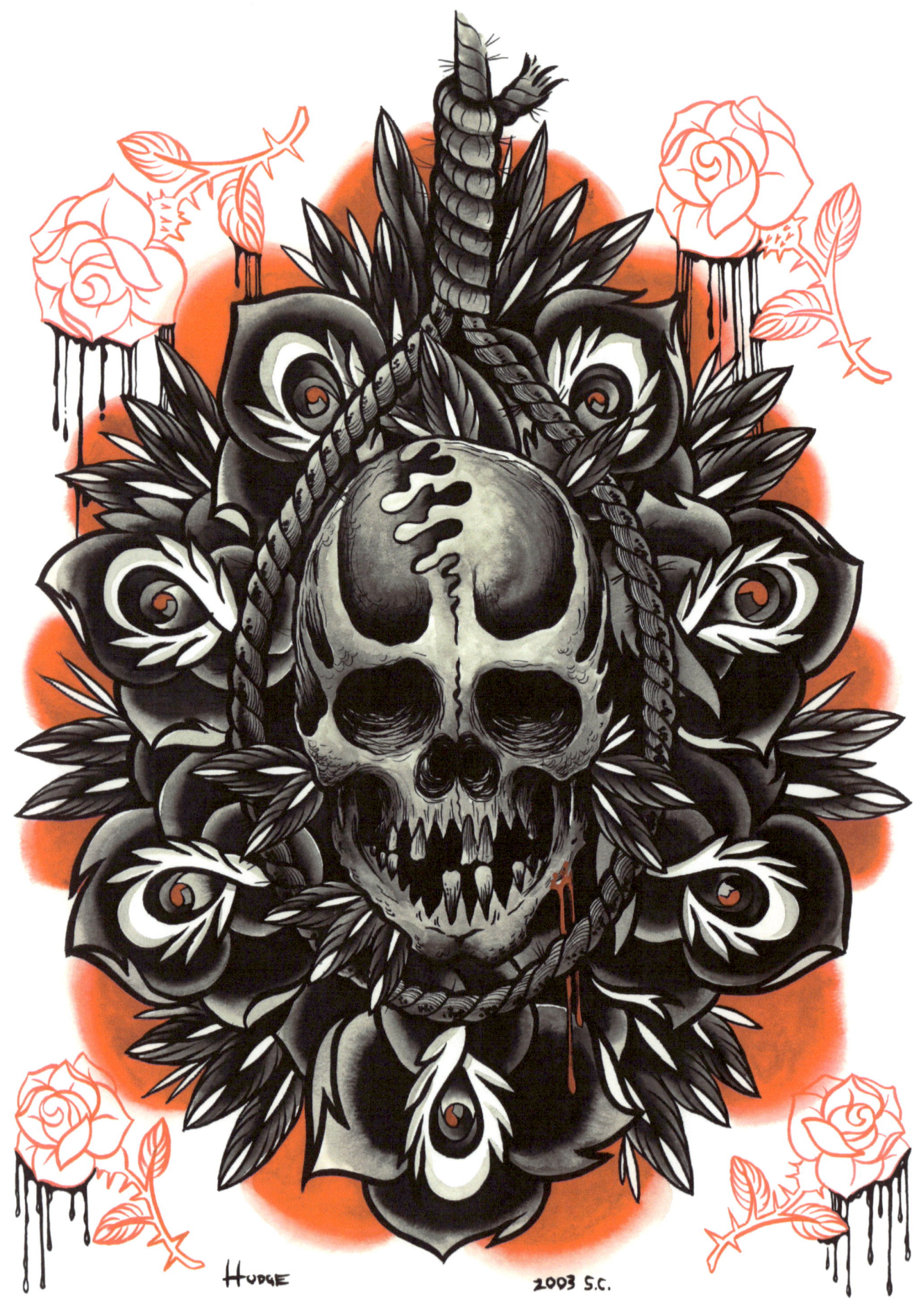

HUDGE   2003 S.C.

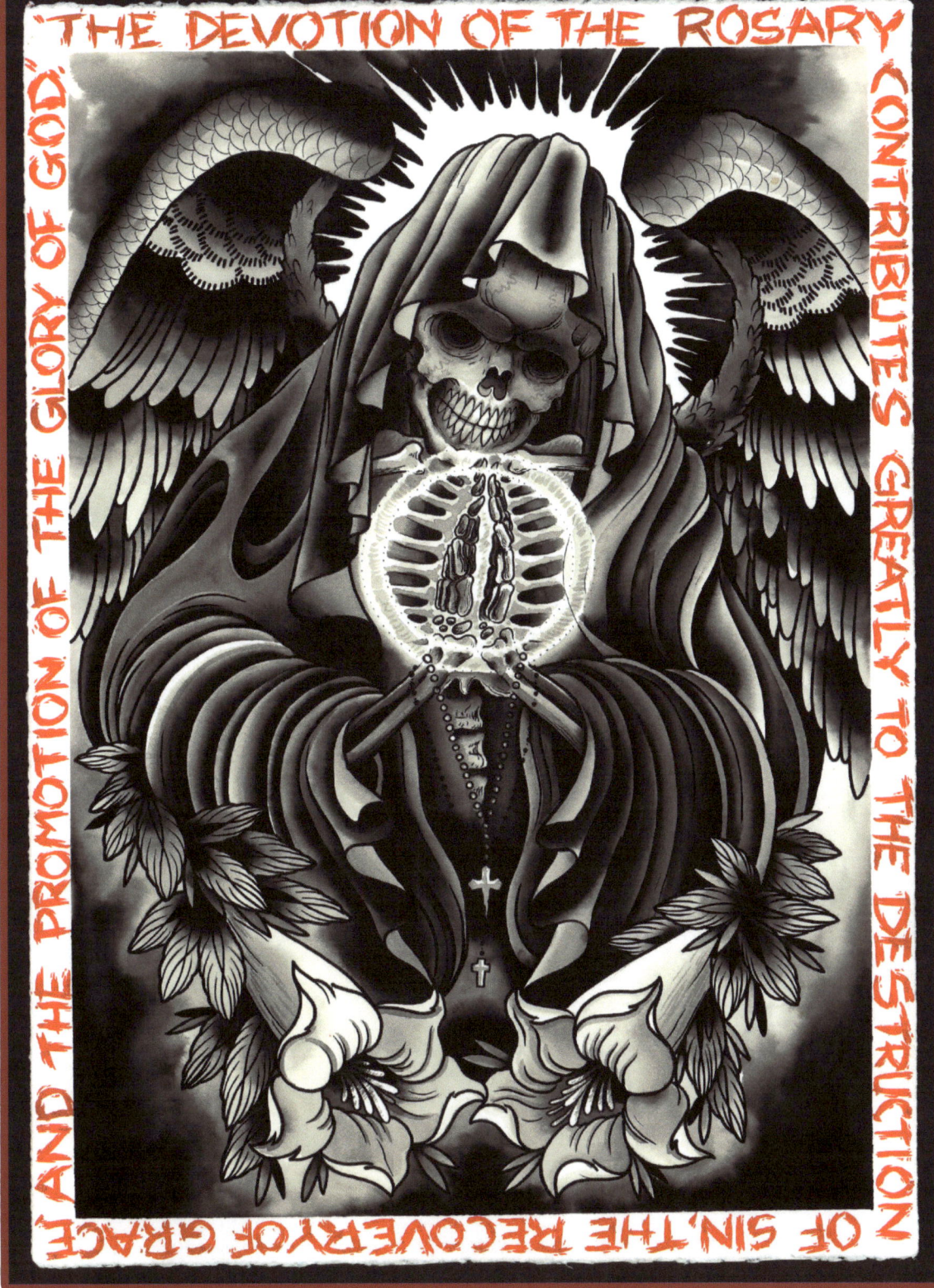

'THE DEVOTION OF THE ROSARY CONTRIBUTES GREATLY TO THE DESTRUCTION OF SIN, THE RECOVERY OF GRACE AND THE PROMOTION OF THE GLORY OF GOD'

Lee Hanna

Aces Tattoo 681 S. Virginia ST Reno, NV 89501
(775) 333-0915
www.acestattoo.com

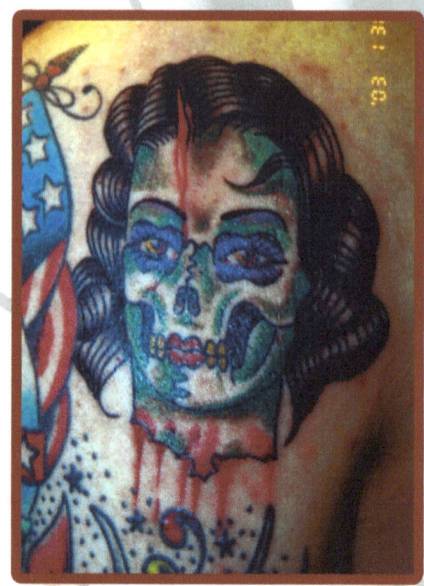

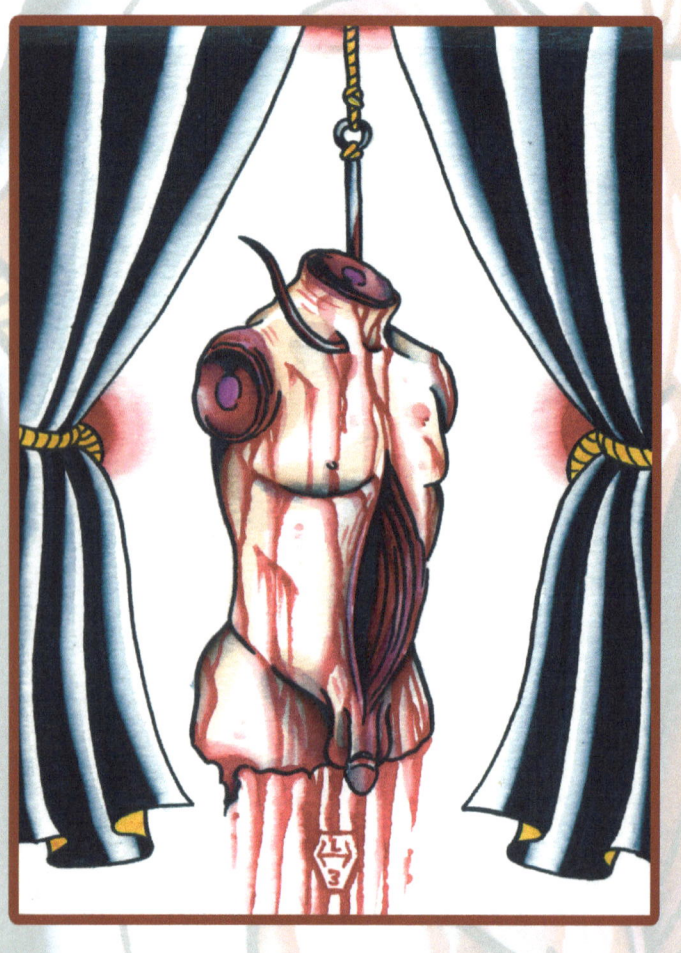

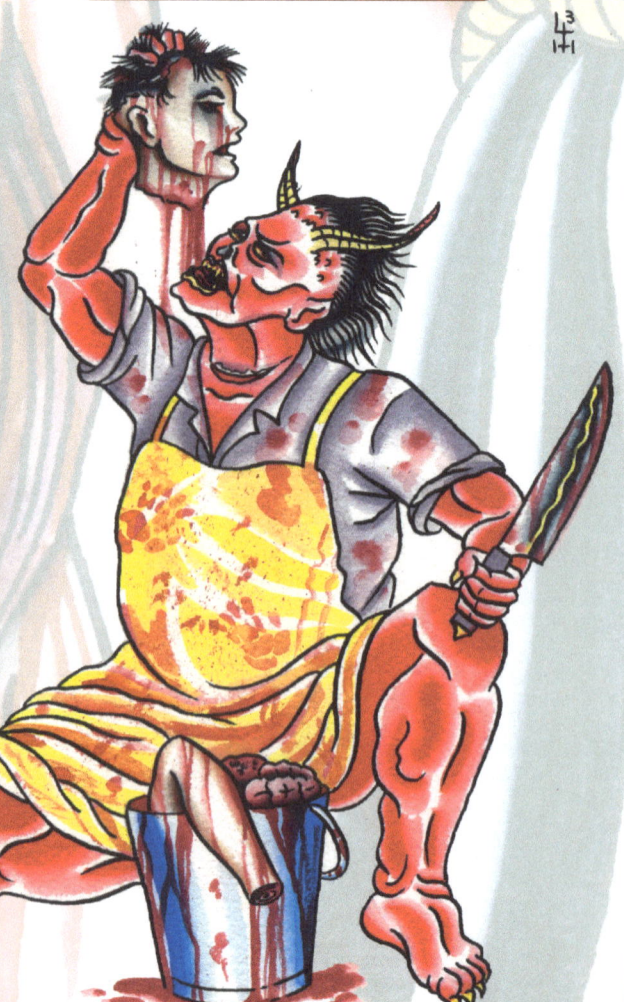

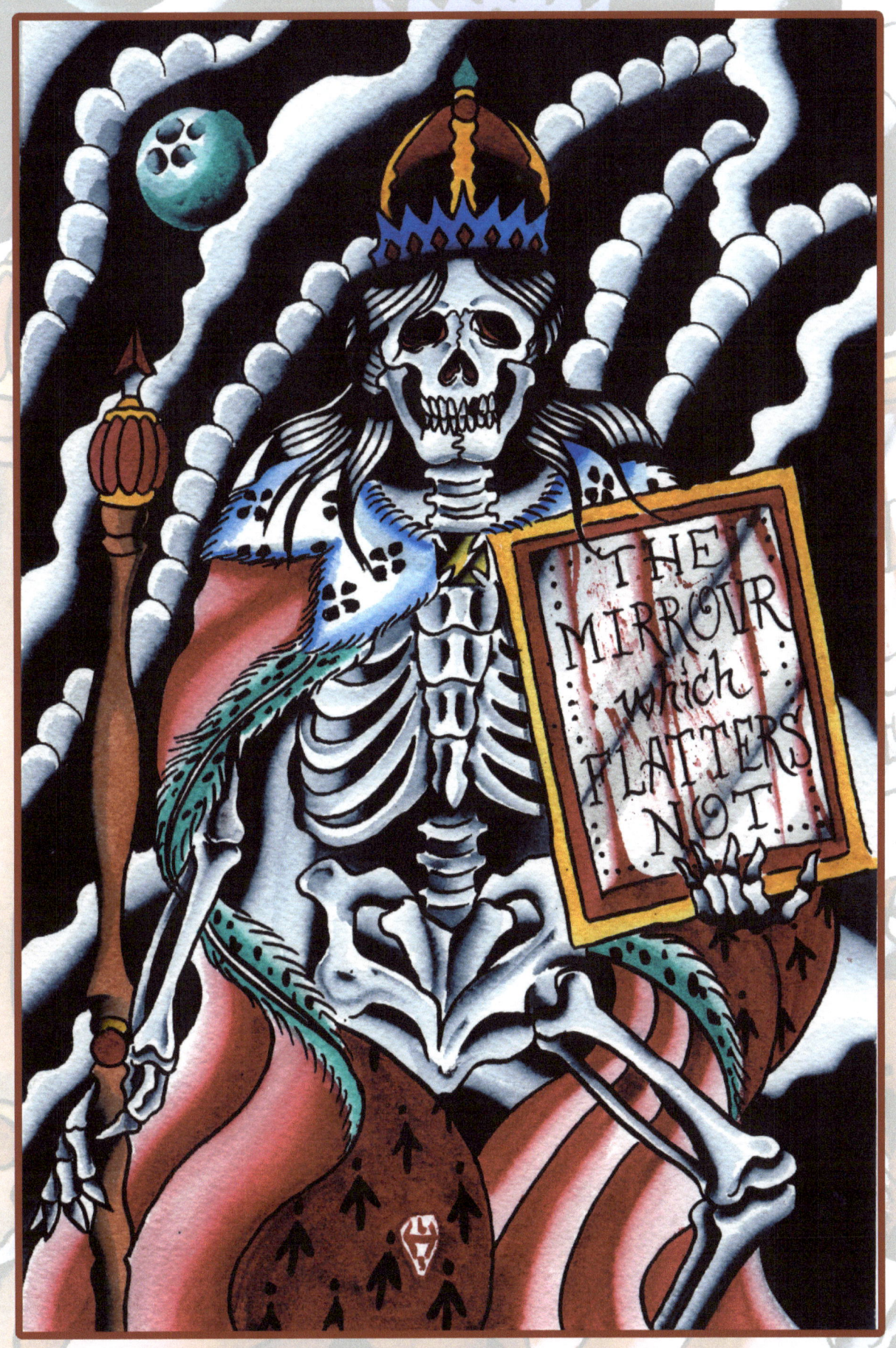

BJ Betts

Lucky Budda Tattoo 722 Philadelphia Pike
Wilmington, DE 19809
(302)420-6010

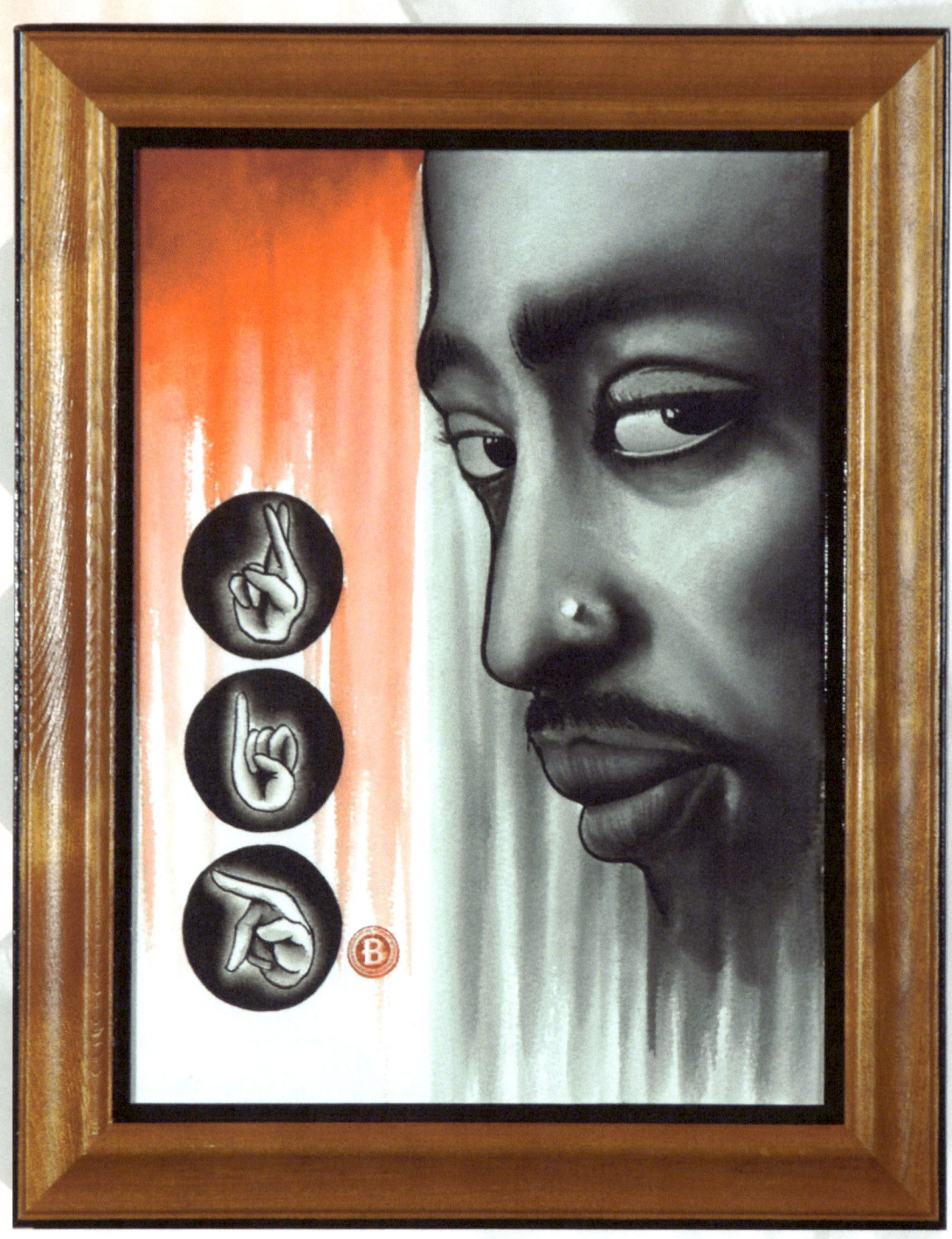

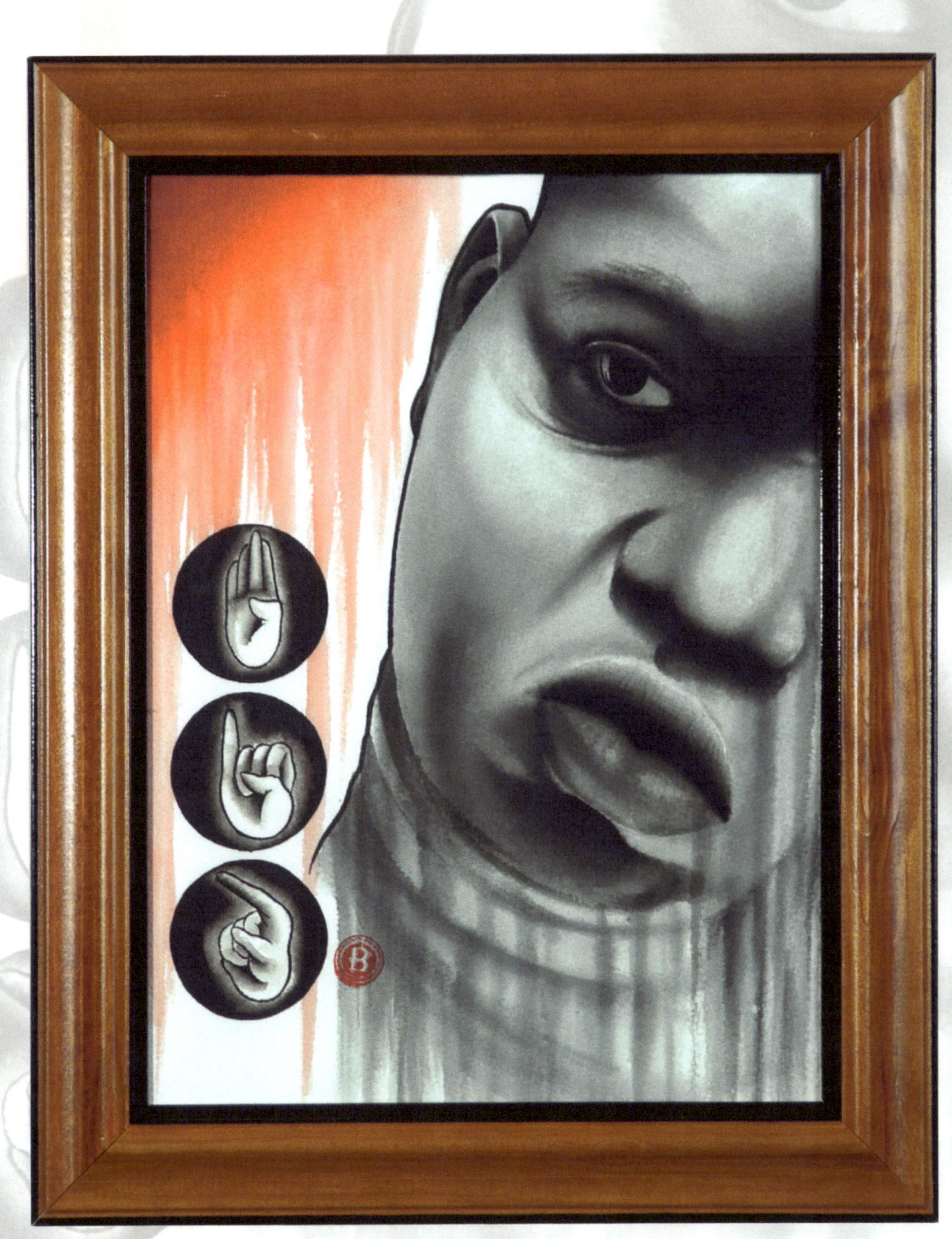

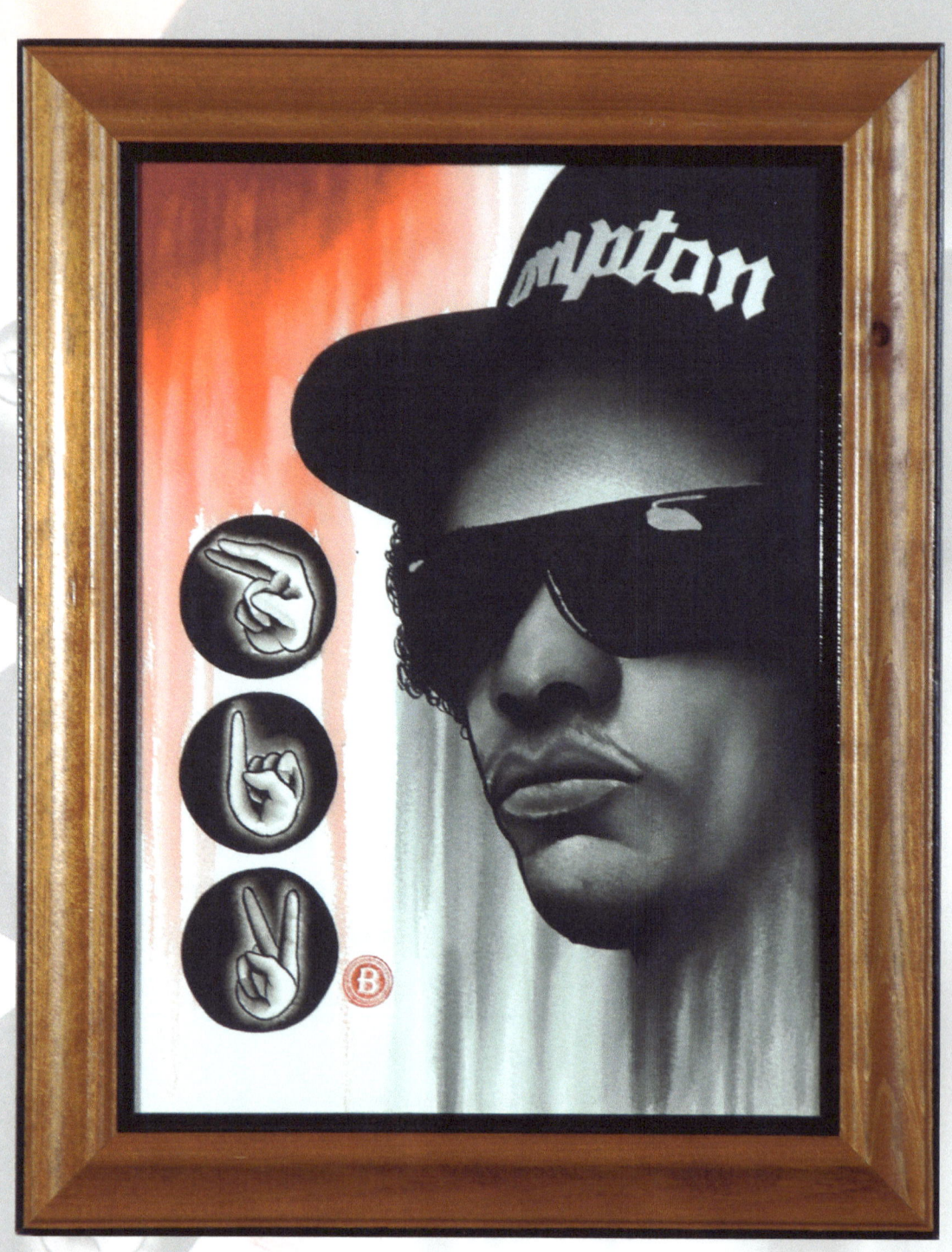

Jason Freeman

Aces Tattoo 681 S. Virginia St. Reno, NV 89501
(775) 333-0915
www.acestattoo.com

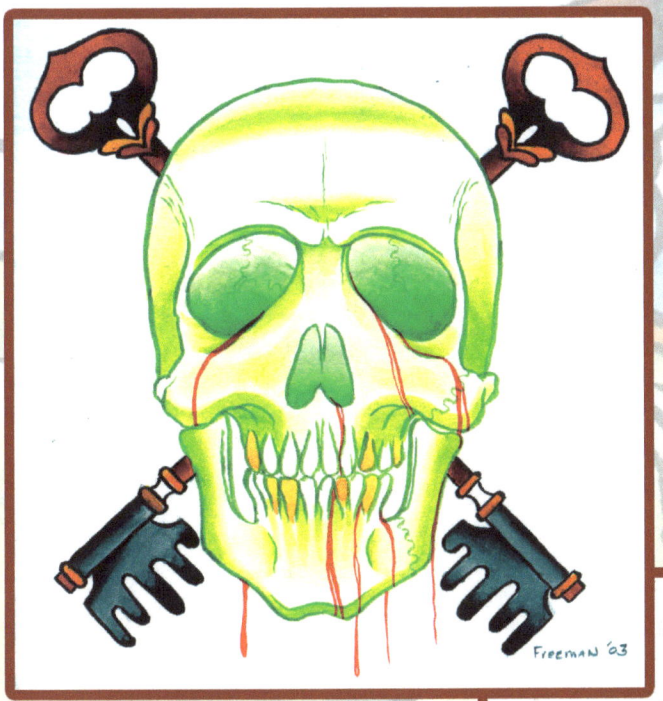

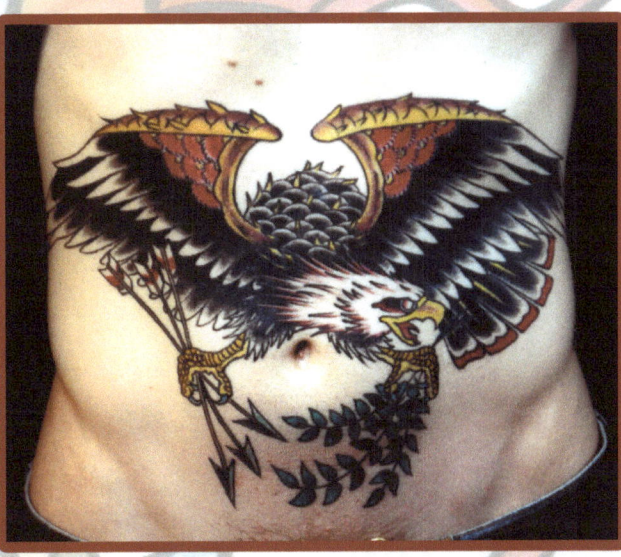

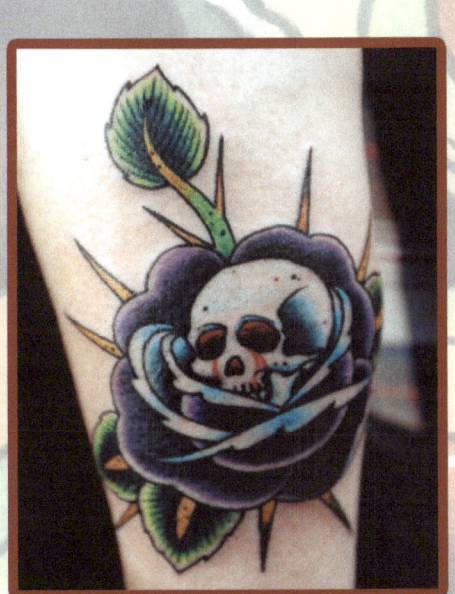

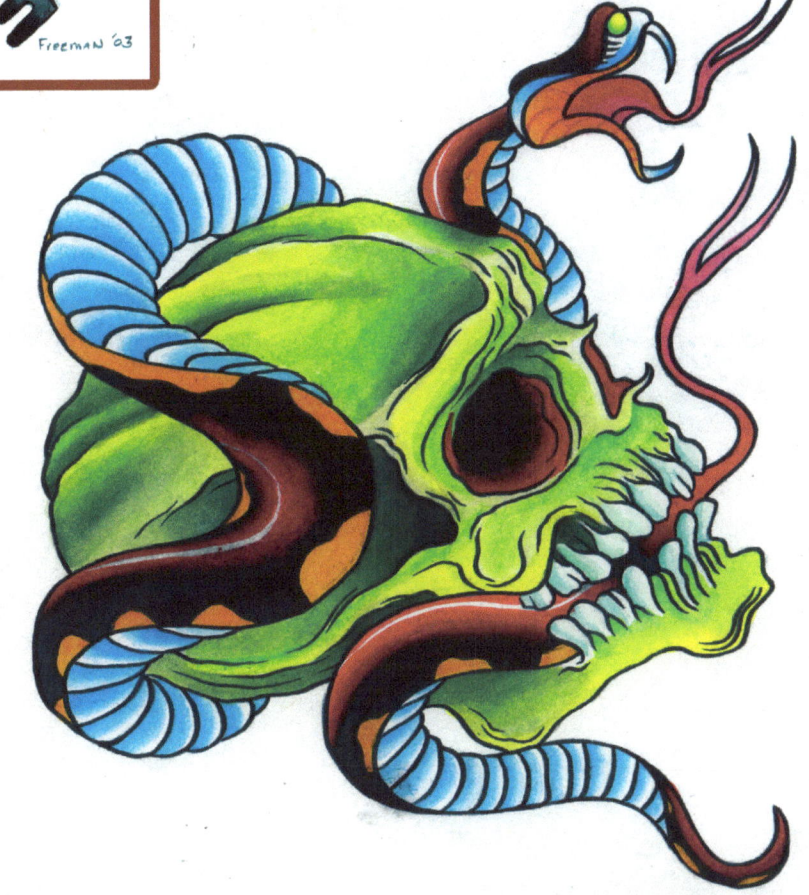

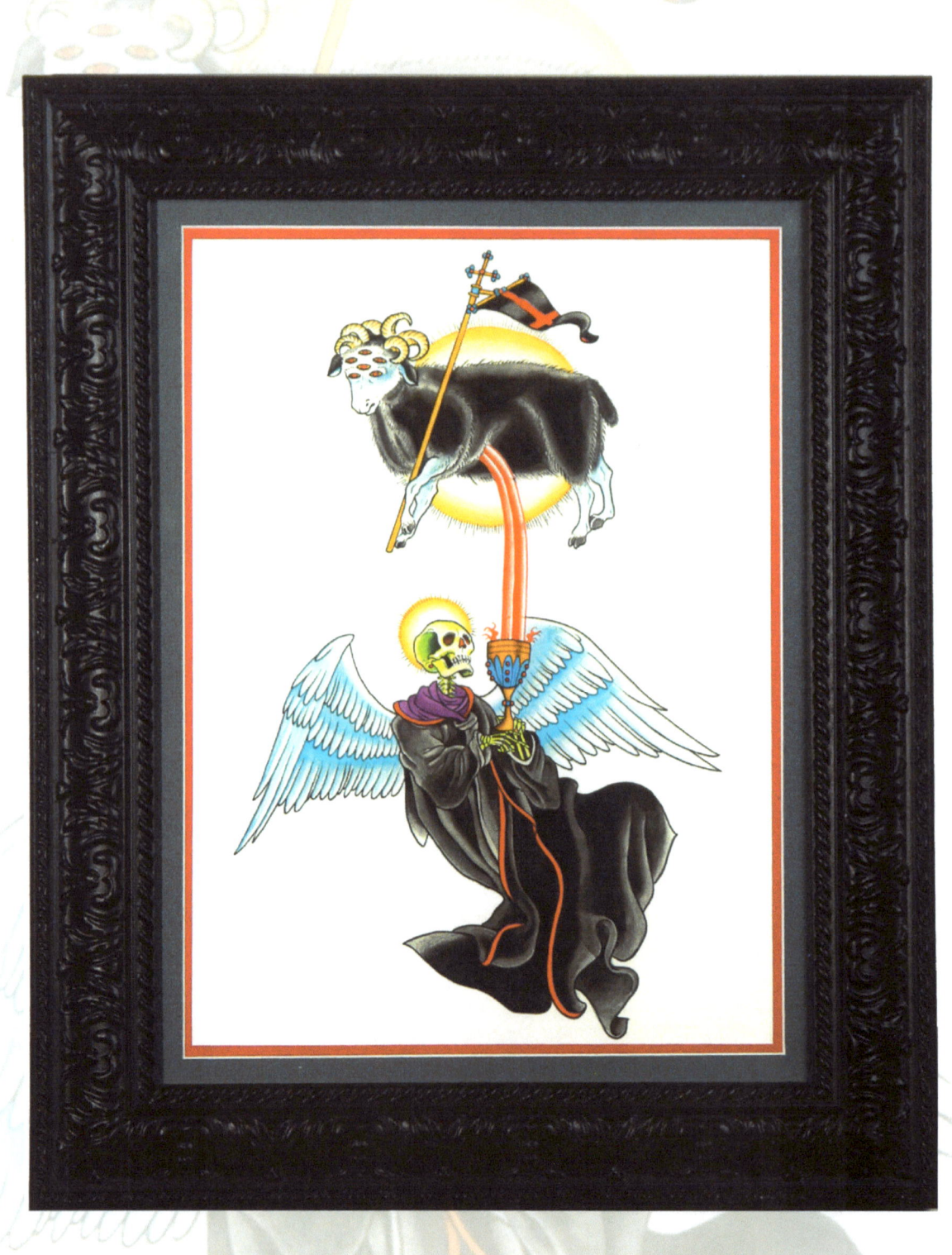

Matt Shamah

New Skool Tattoo 306 S 3Rd ST San Jose, CA 95112
(408)279-0927
www.newskooltattoo.com

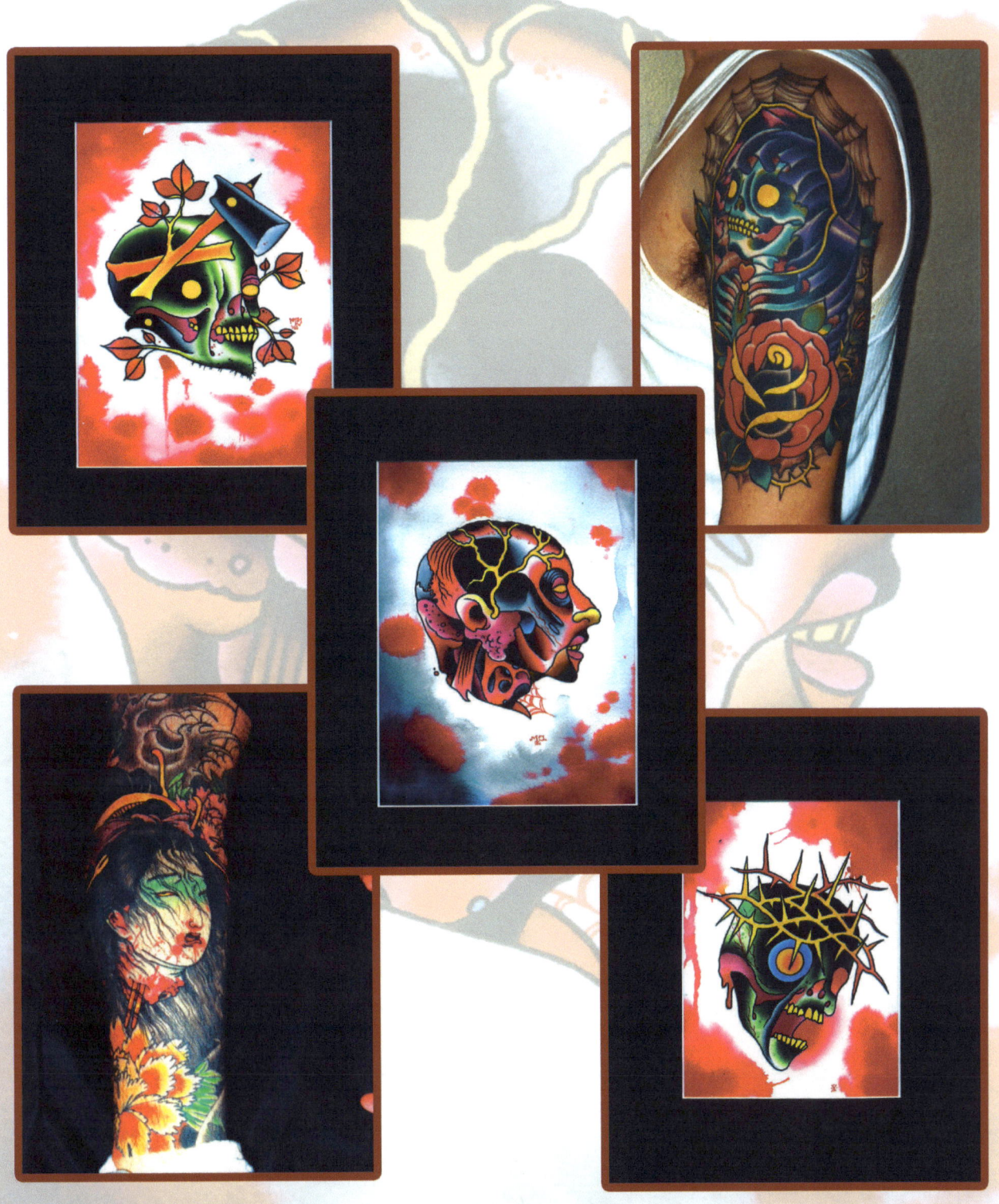

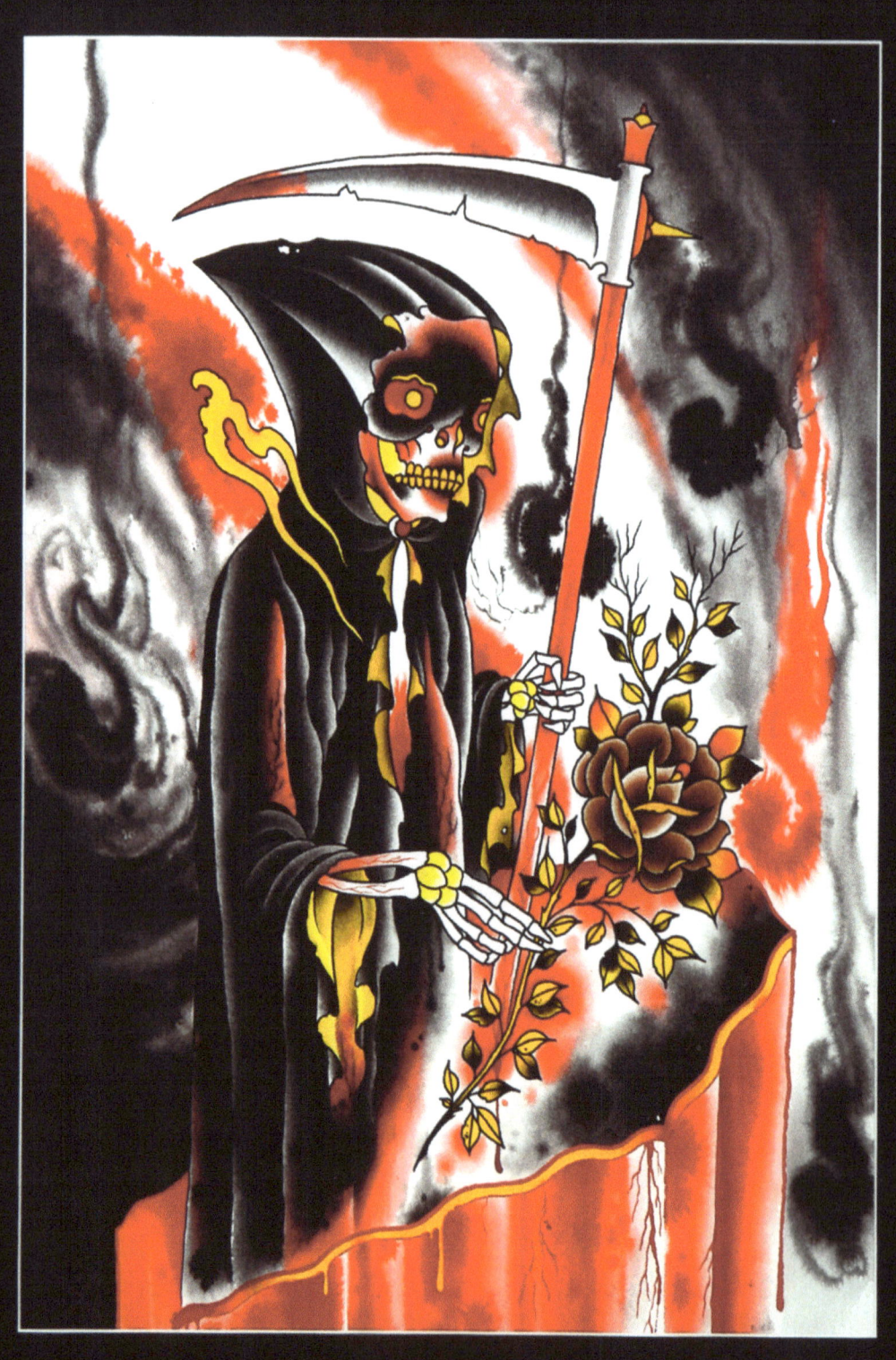

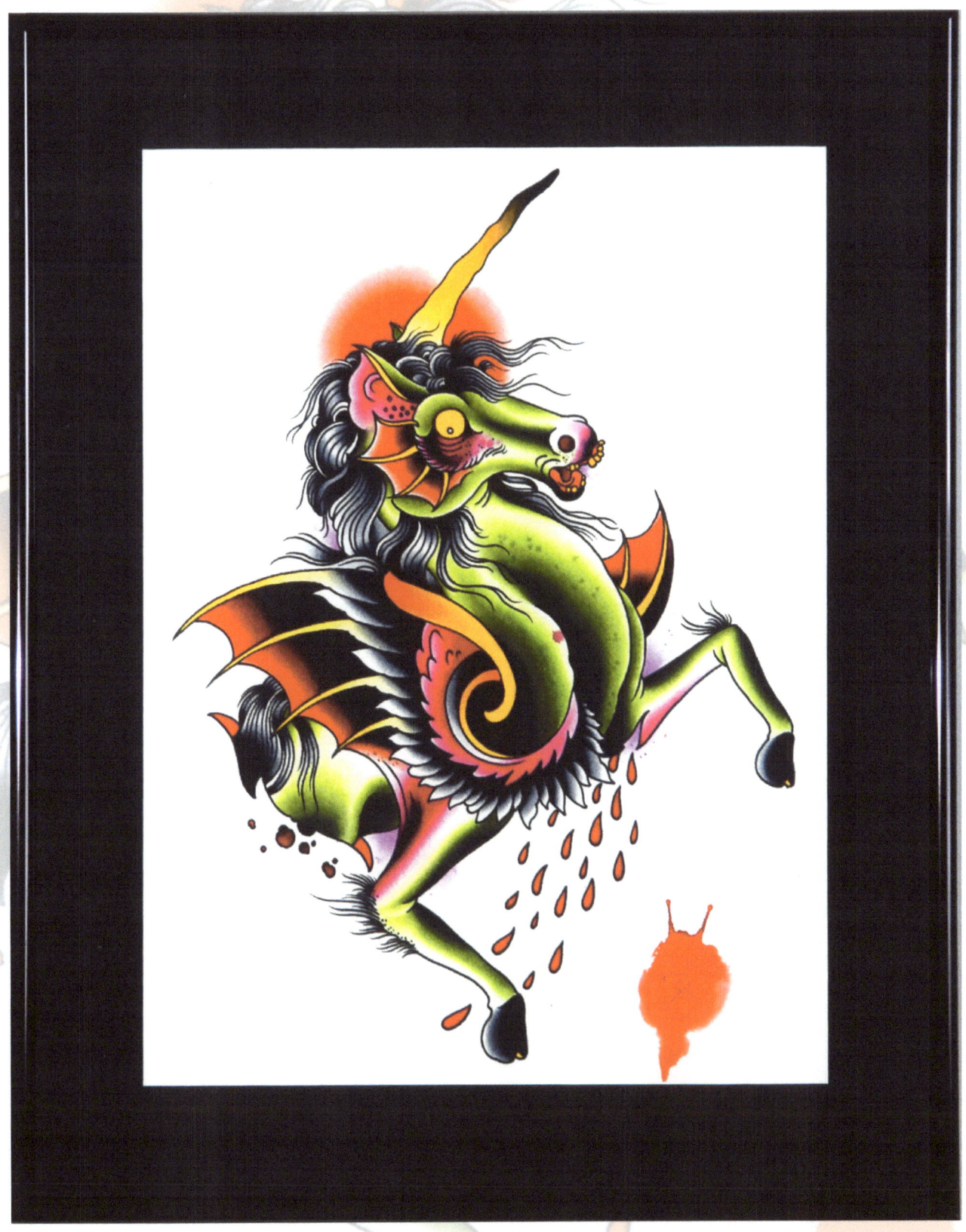

Grady Spades

Full Color Coverage
24B Defense Street Annapolis, MD 21401
410-224-0992
www.gradyspades.com

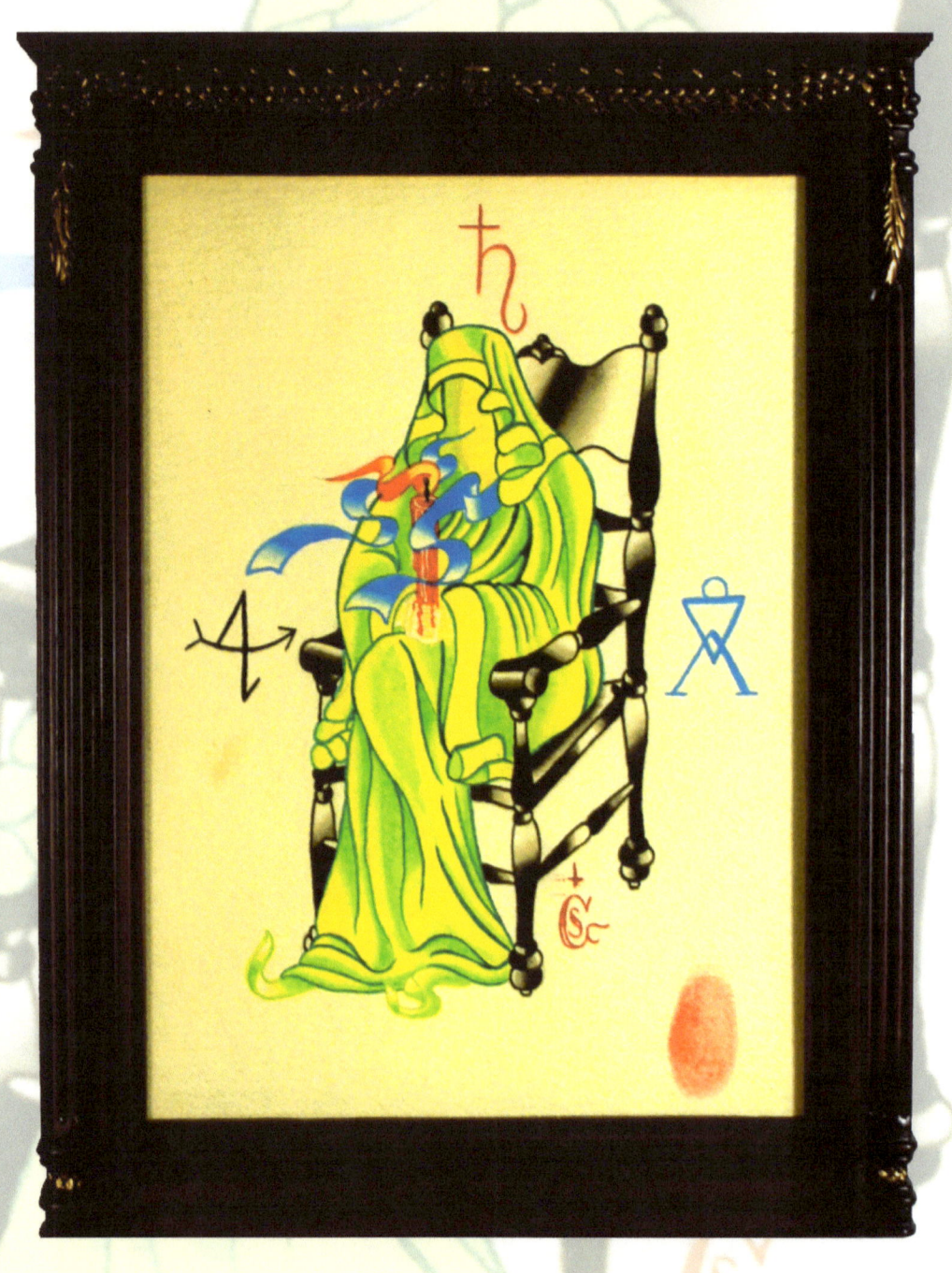

Rex Barnes

Blue Flame Tattoo 3015 Hillsborough St. Raleigh, NC 27606
(919) 755-3355

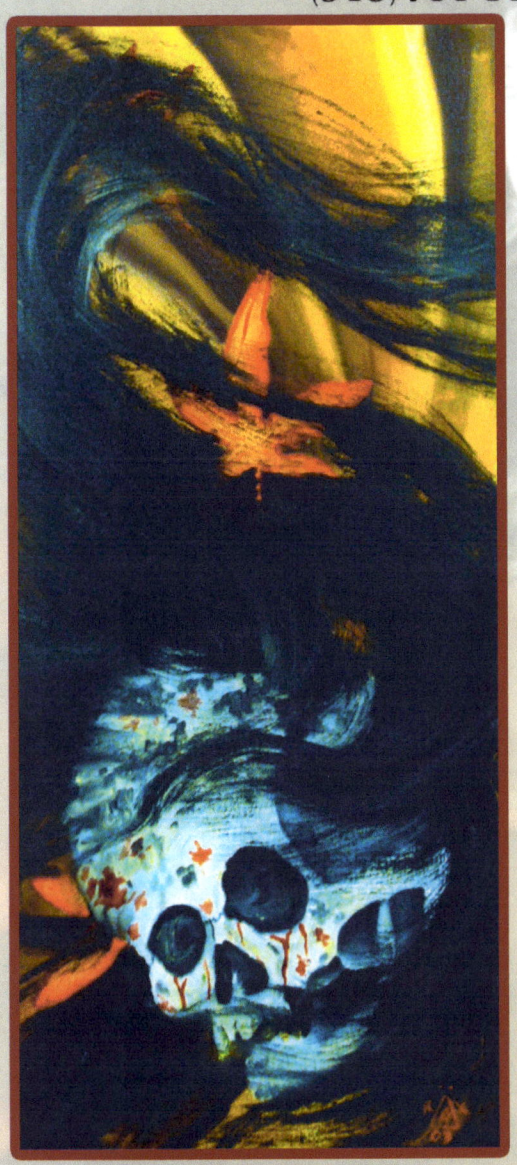

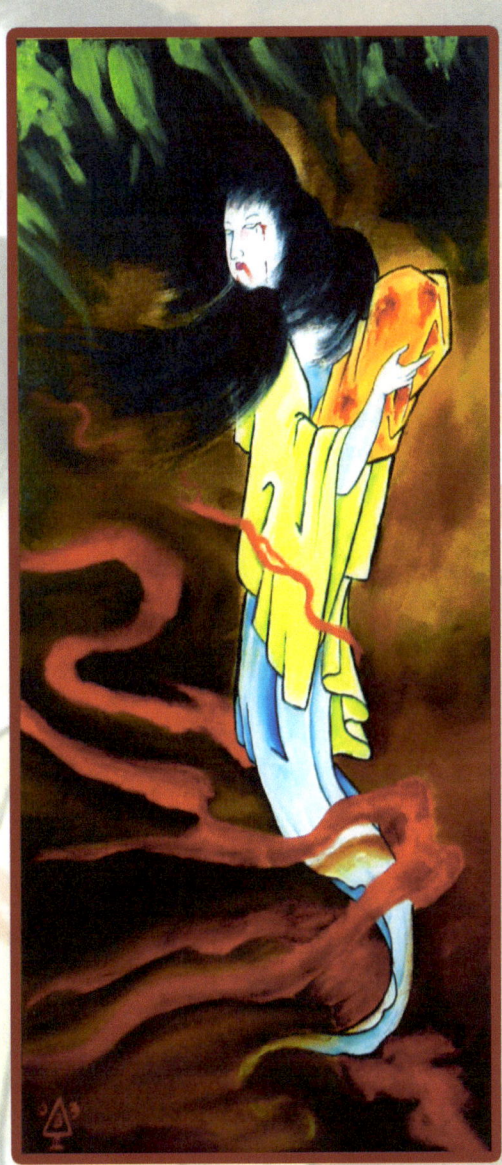

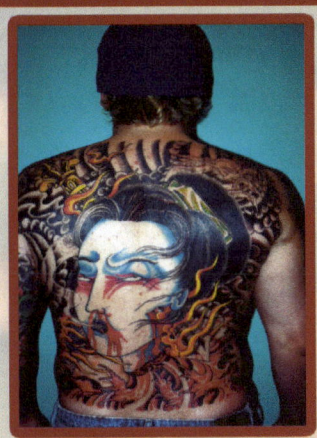

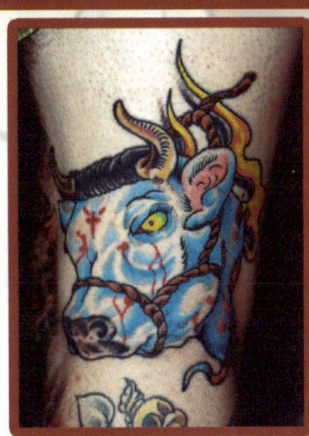

Flip

True Art
1430 Soquel Avenue, Santa Cruz, CA 95062
(831) 426-8783

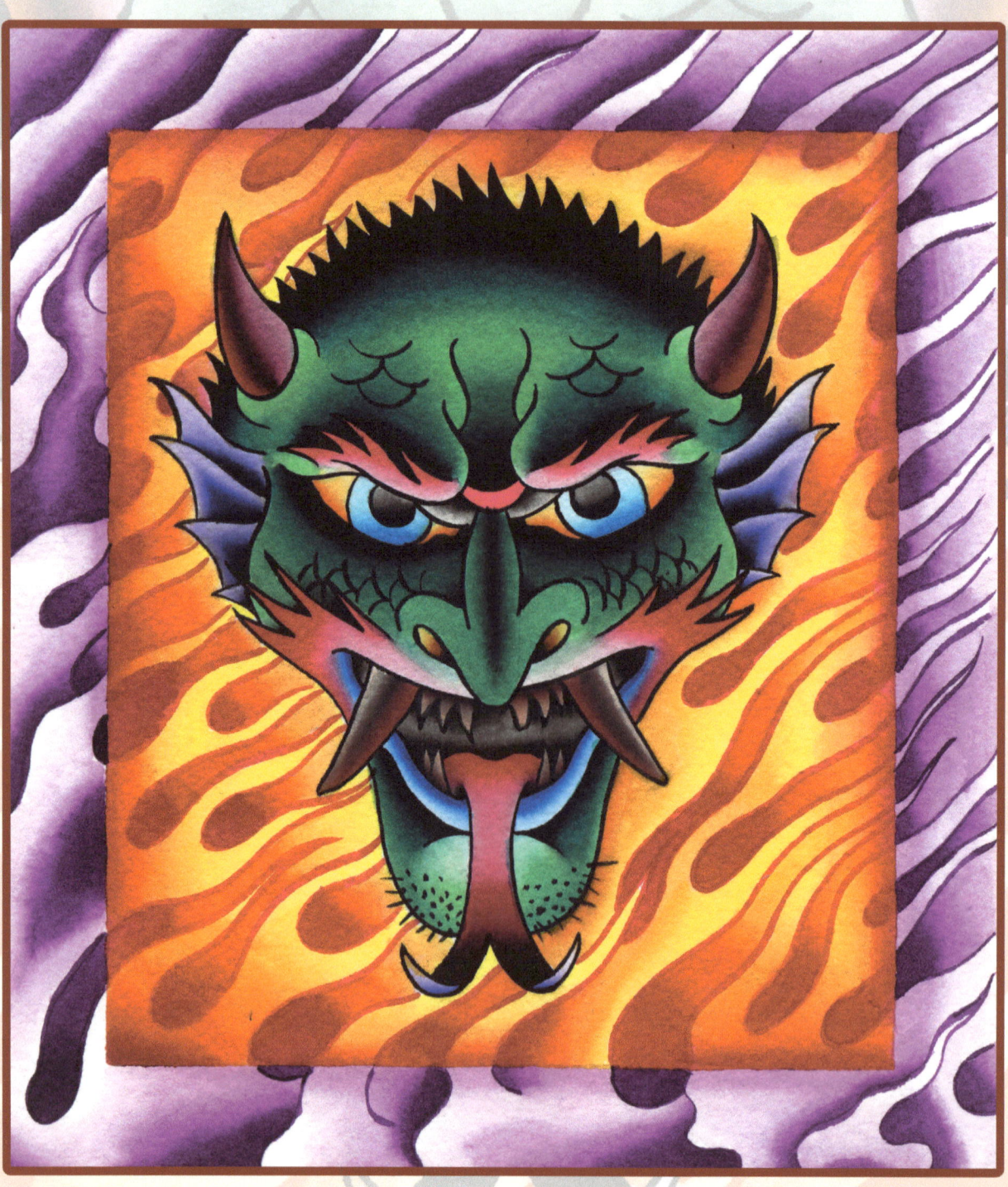

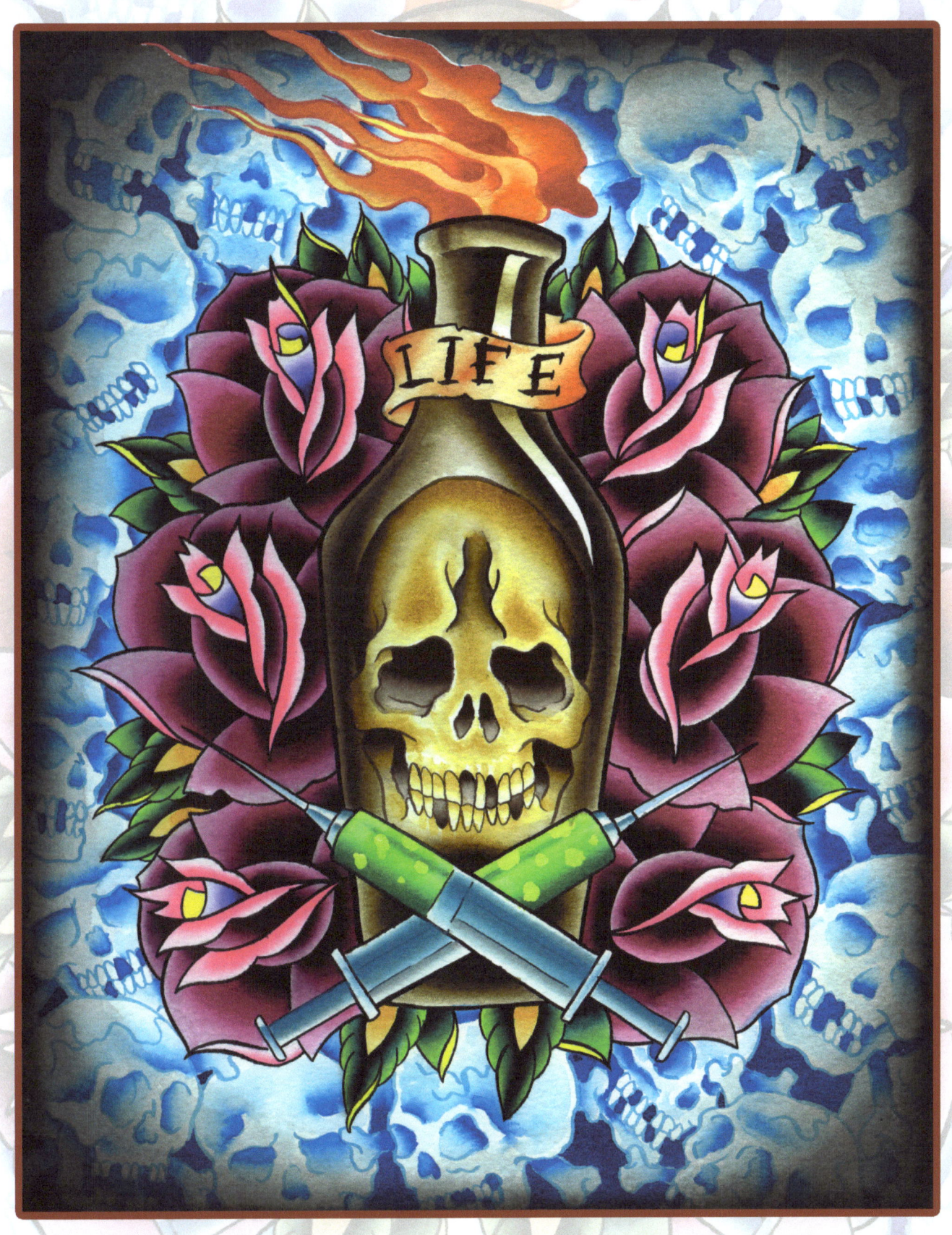

Cory Lenherr

Club Tattoo 1212 E. Apache Blvd. Ste. 104 Tempe, AZ 85281
(480) 902-0943
www.clubtattoo.com

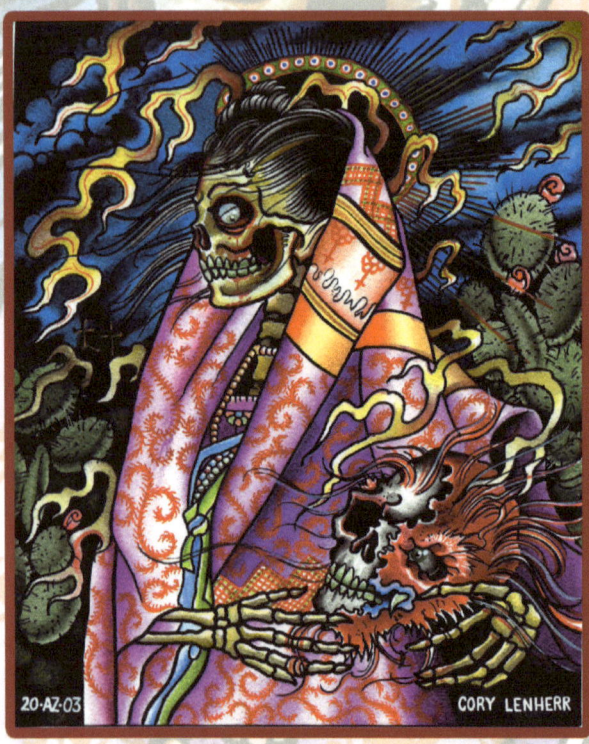

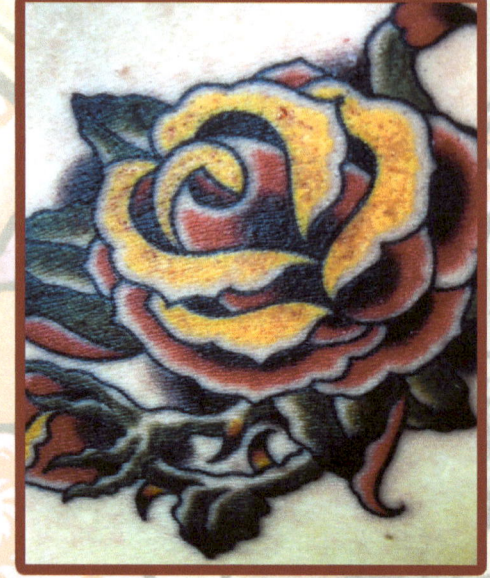

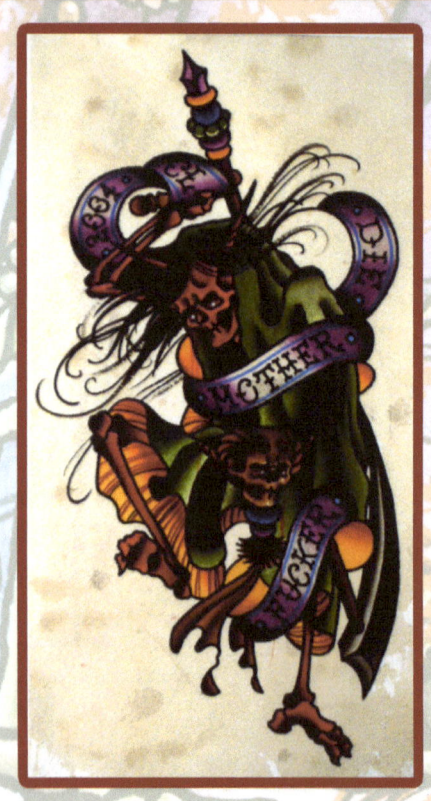

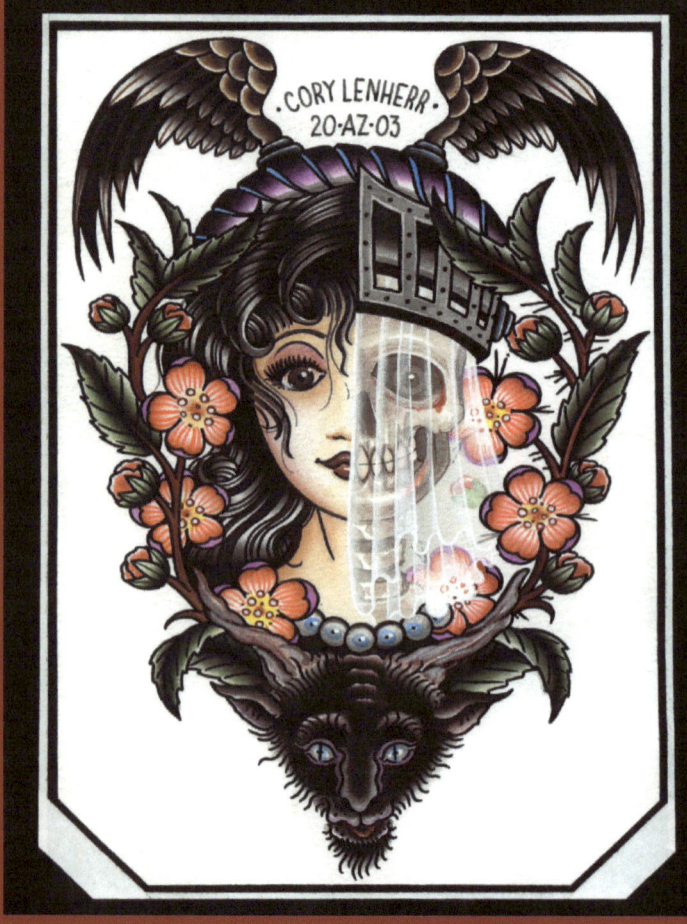

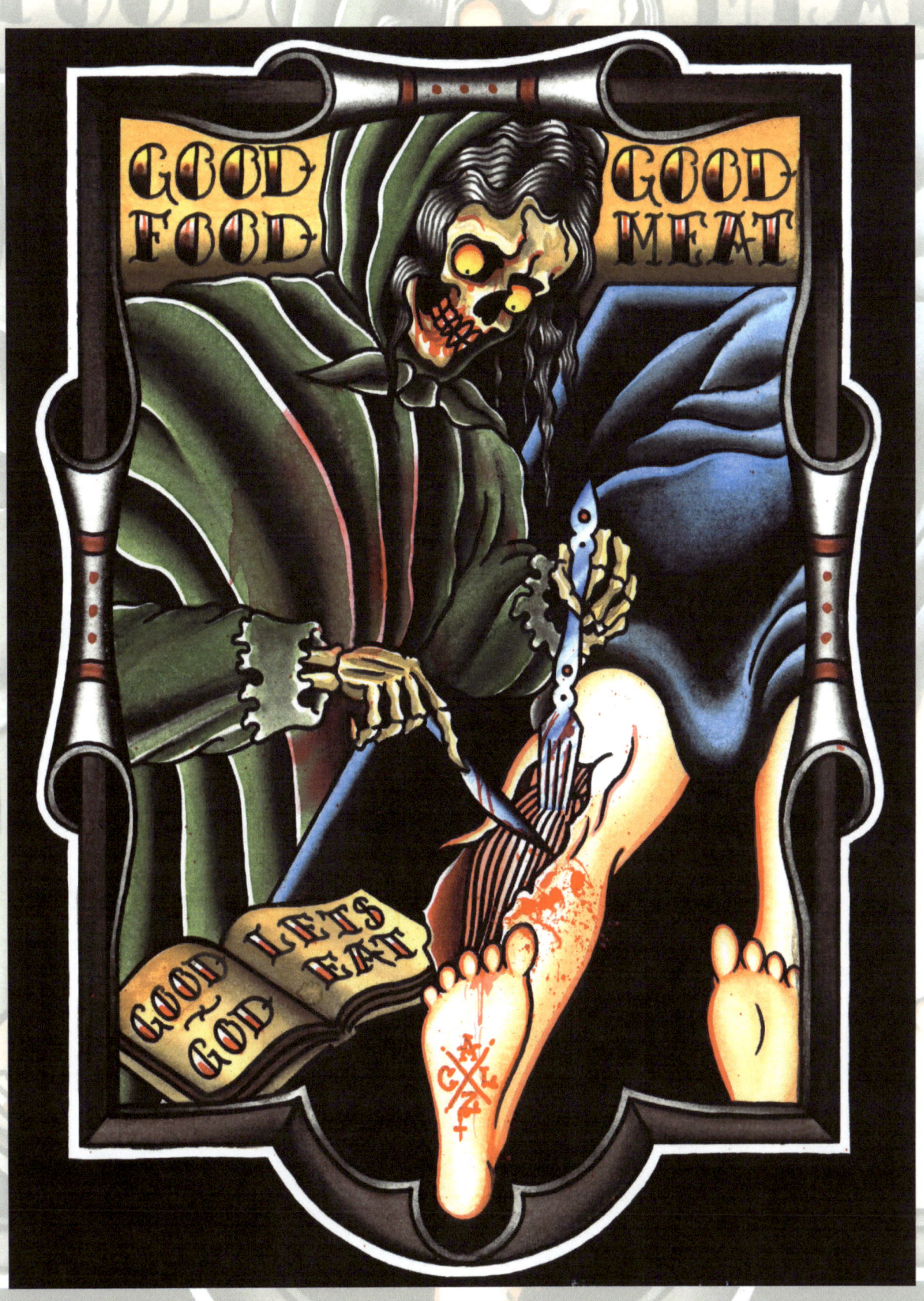

Claudia Baca

St. Sabrina's 2751 Hennepin Ave. Minneapolis, MN 55408
(612) 874-7360
www.billysmind.homestead.com

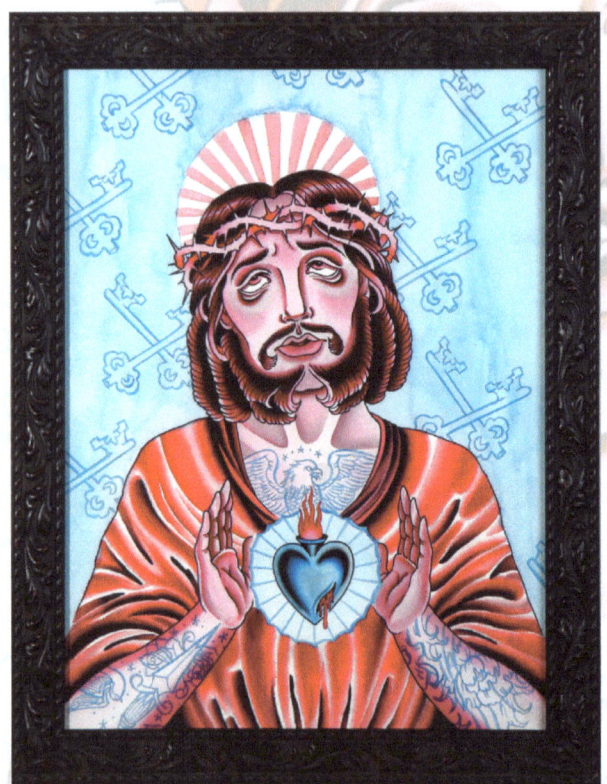

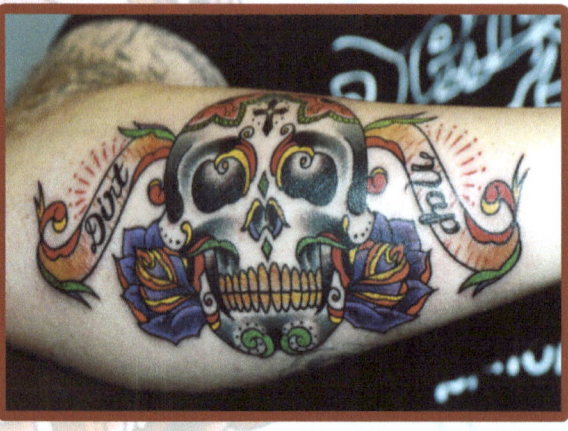

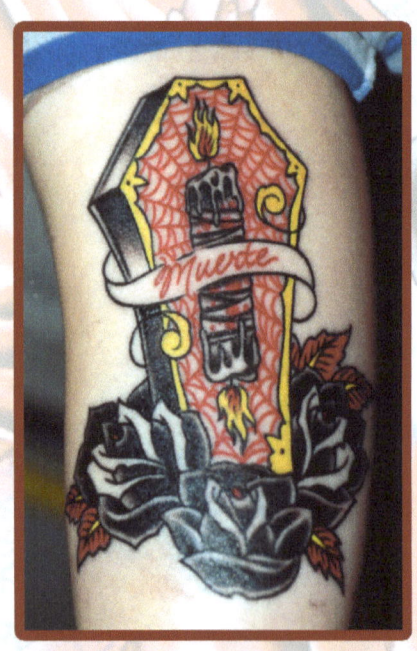

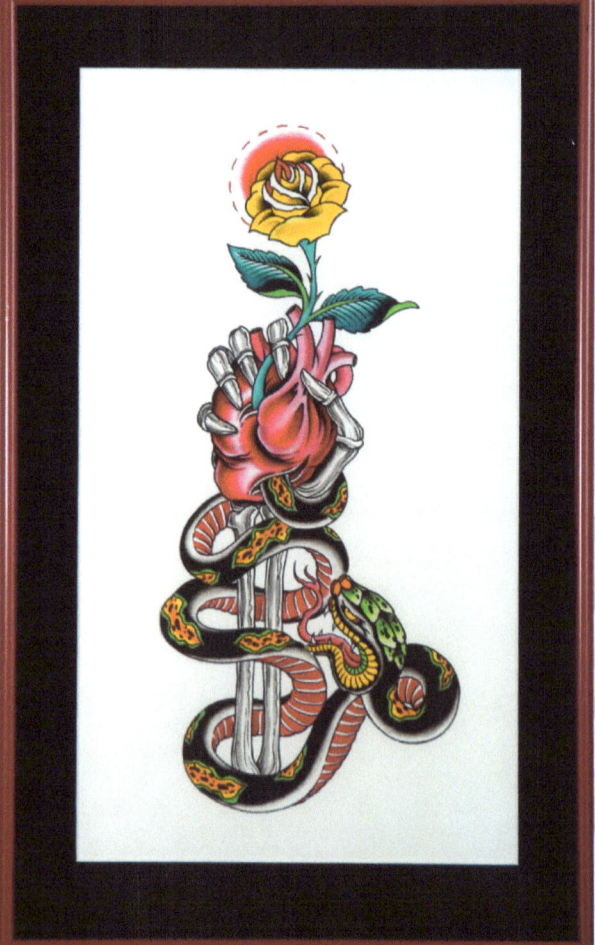

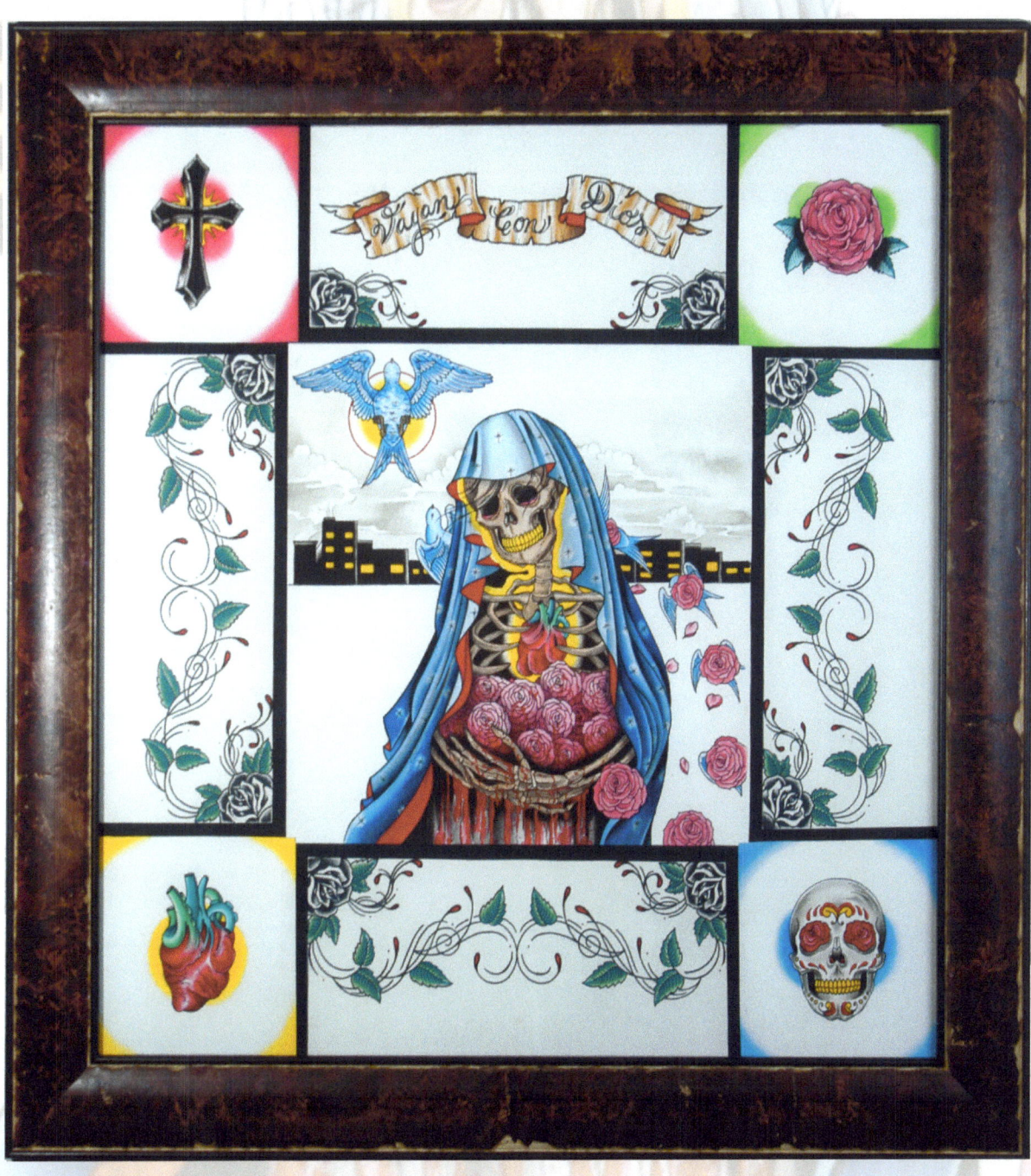

Derrick Snodgrass

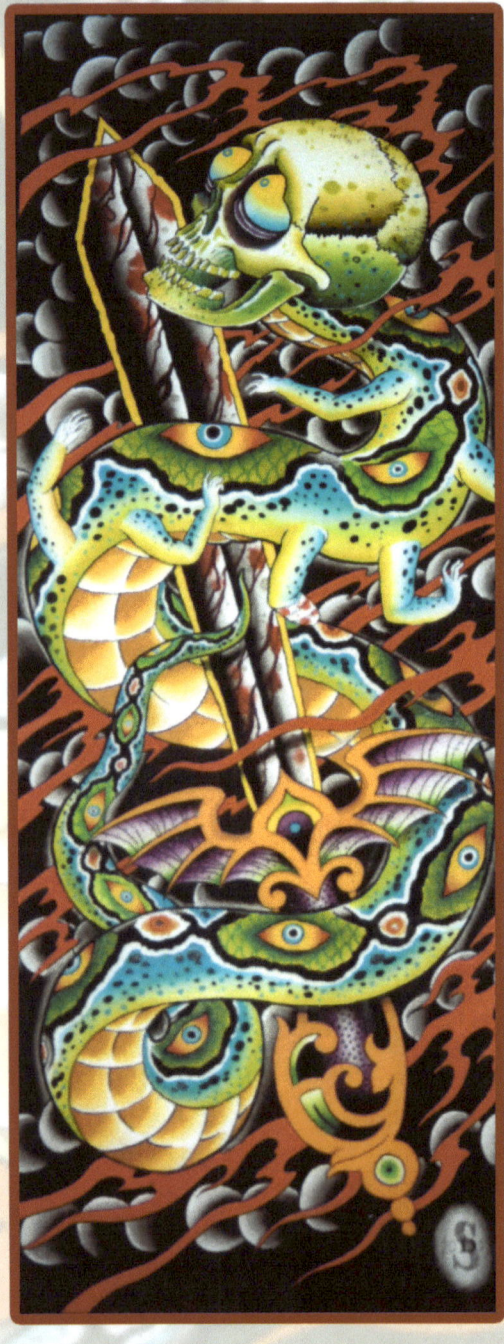
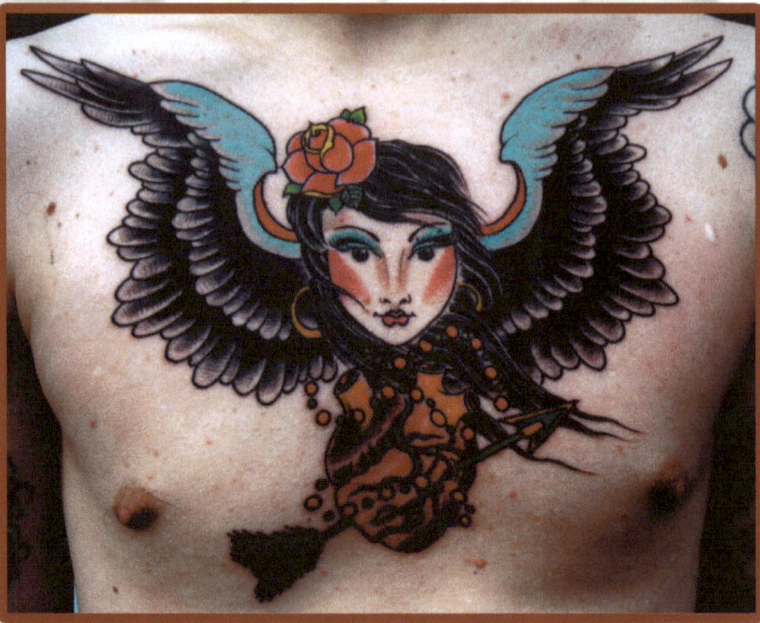
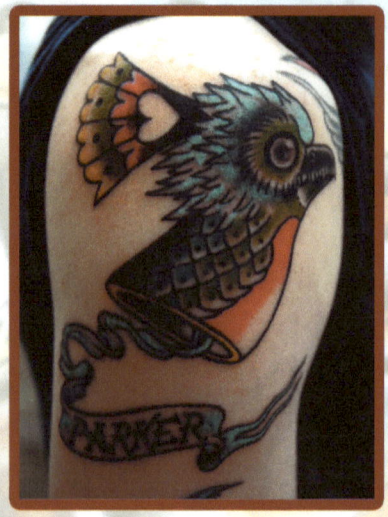
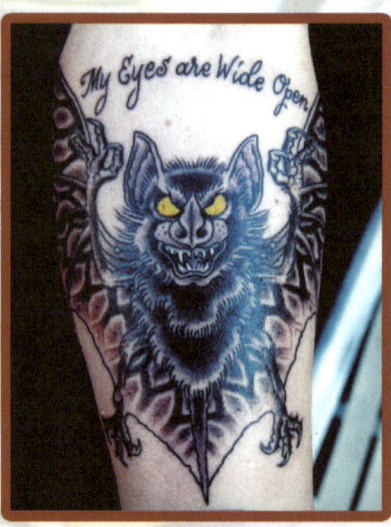

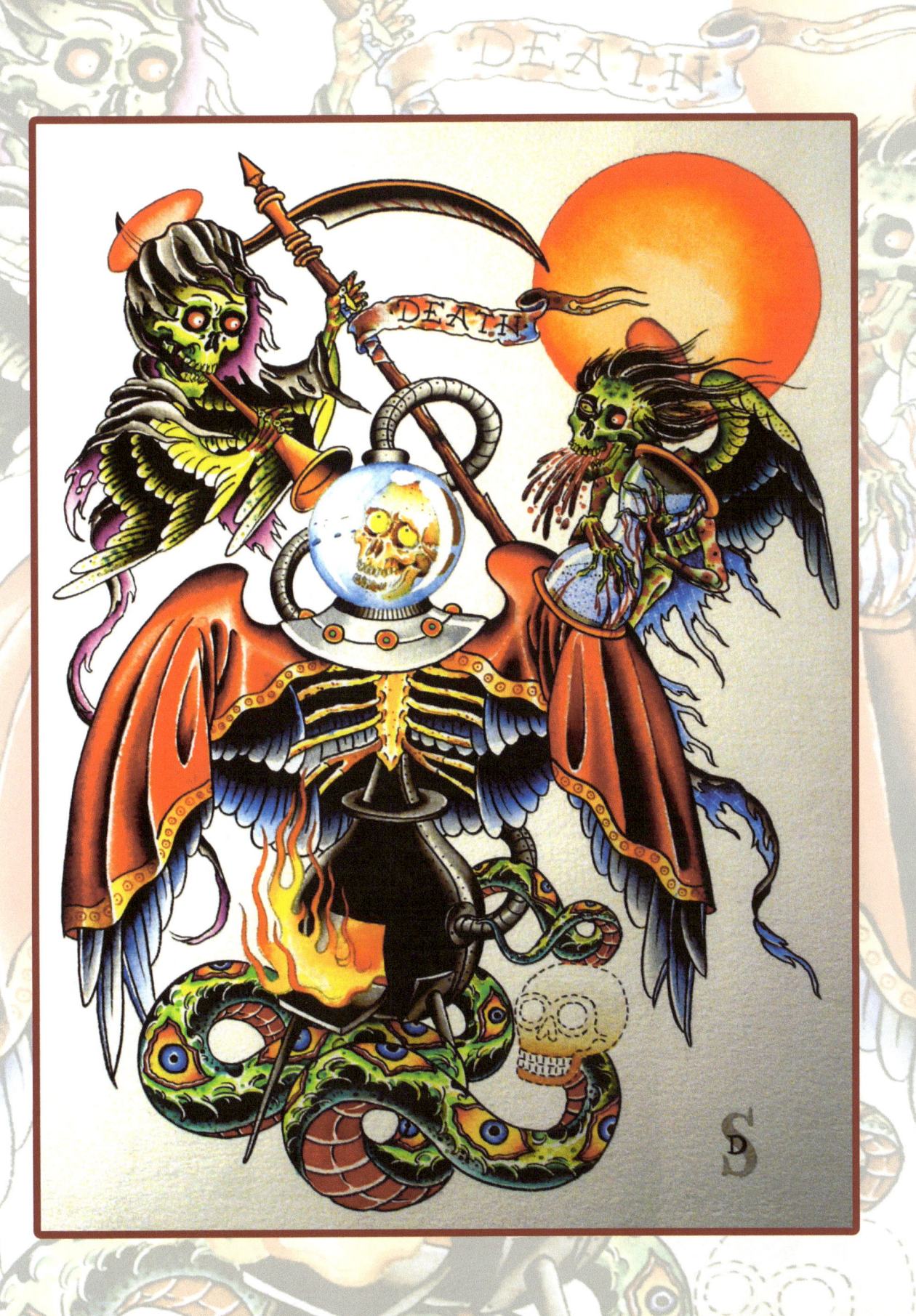

Zack Kinsey

Leviticus Tattoo 4109 E Lake St. Minneapolis, MN
(619) 729-1475
www.leviticustattoo.com

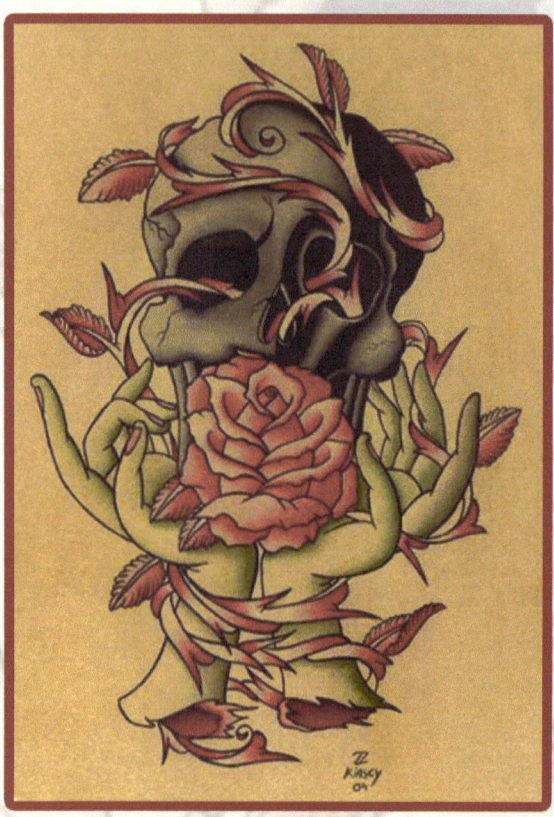

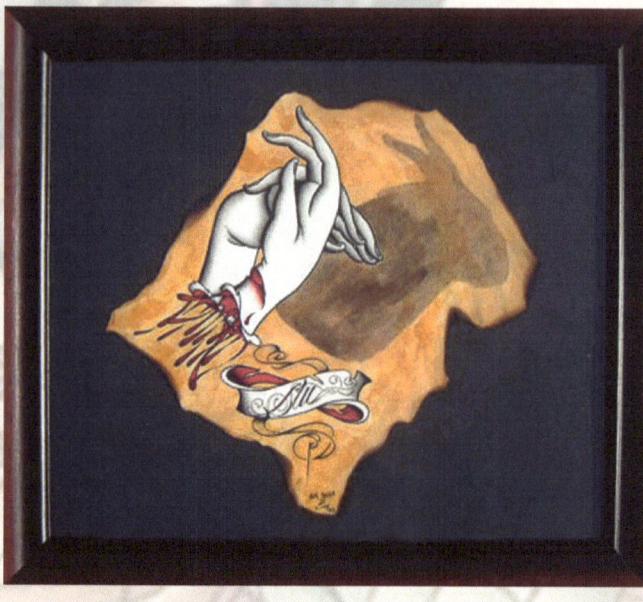

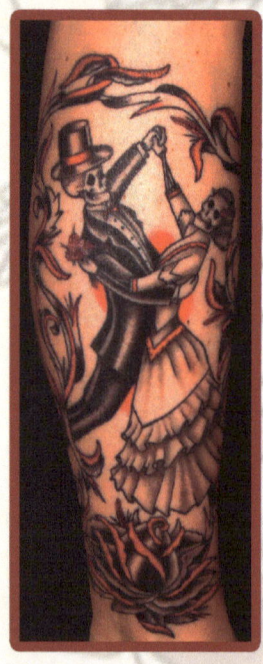

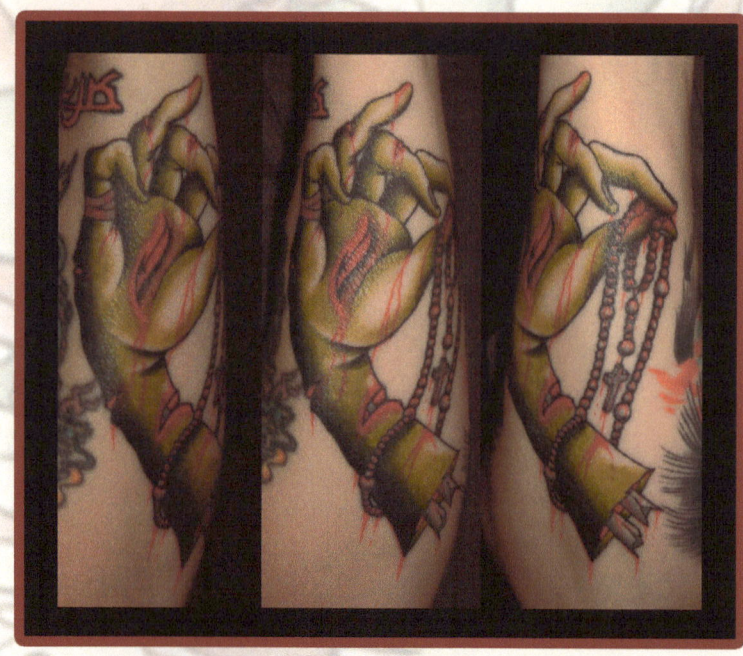

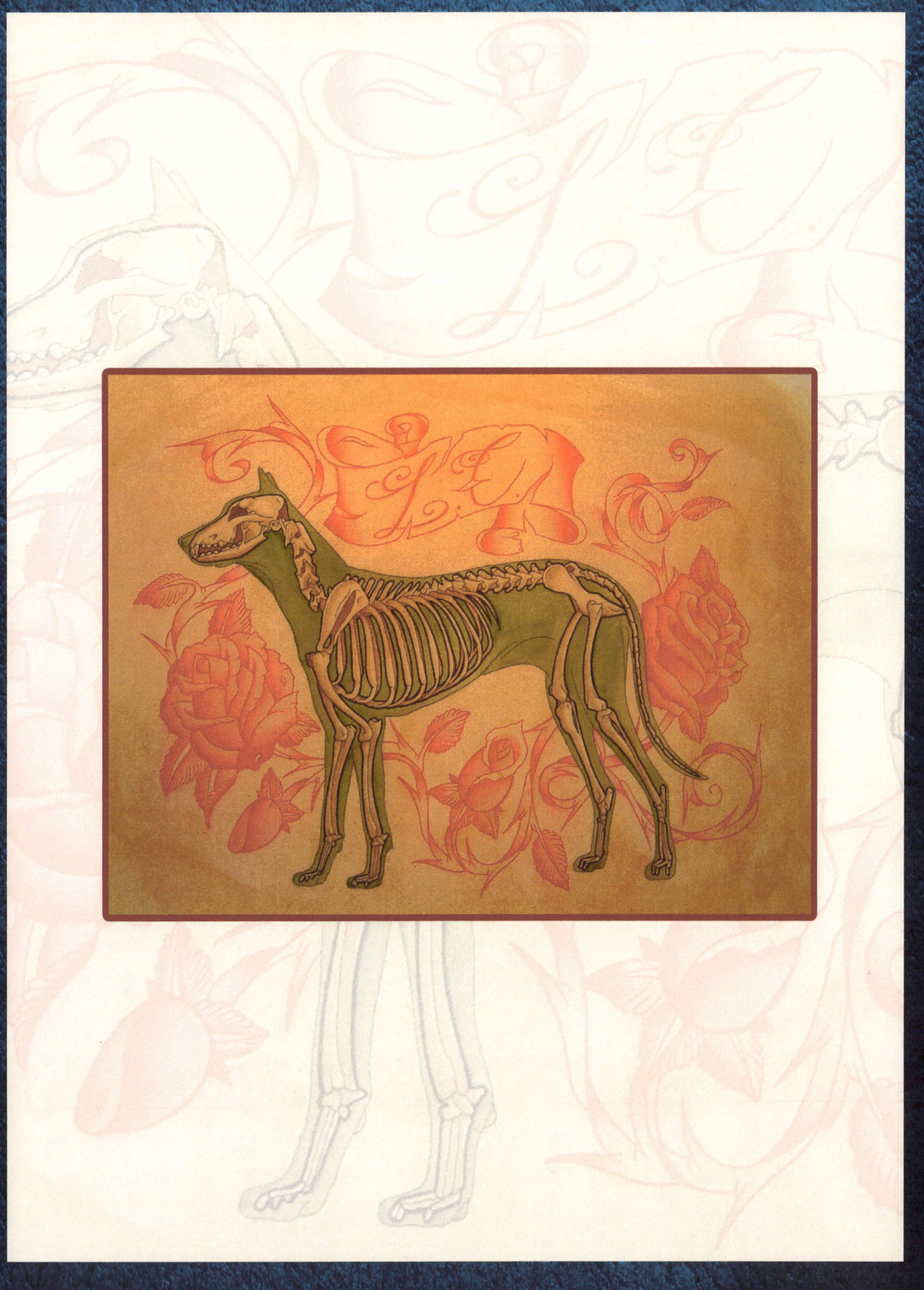

Grez

Redemption Tattoo 2285 Mass. Ave Cambridge, MA 02140
(617) 576-0097
www.redemptiontattoo.com

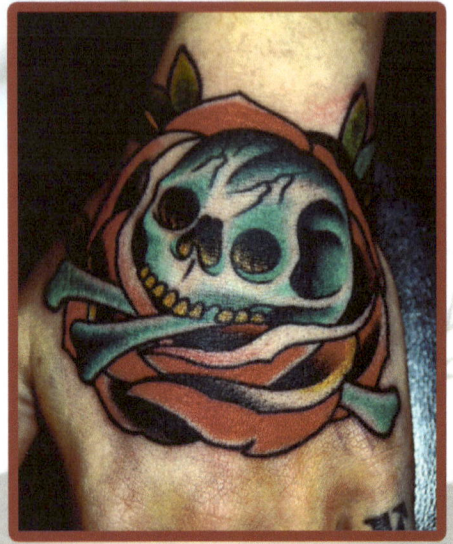

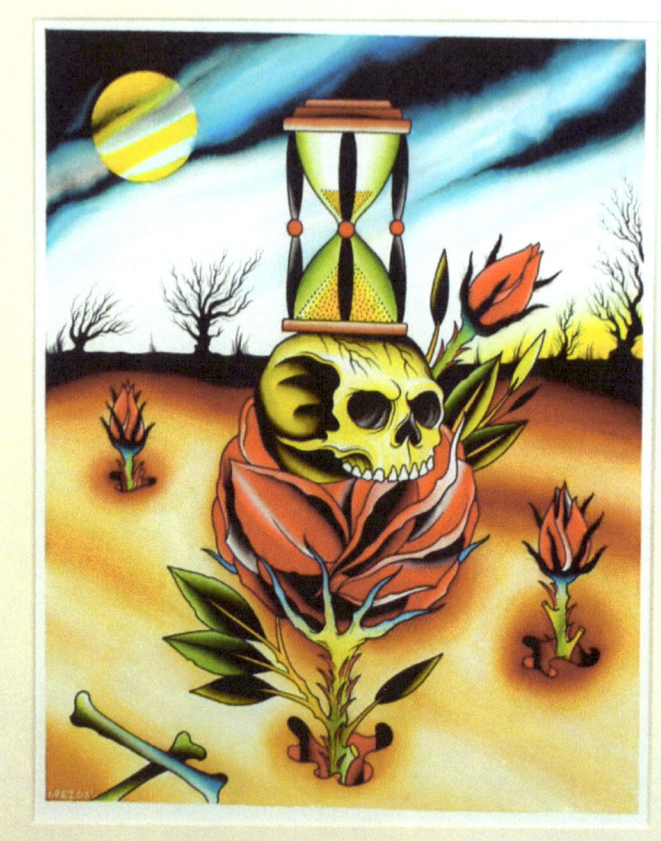

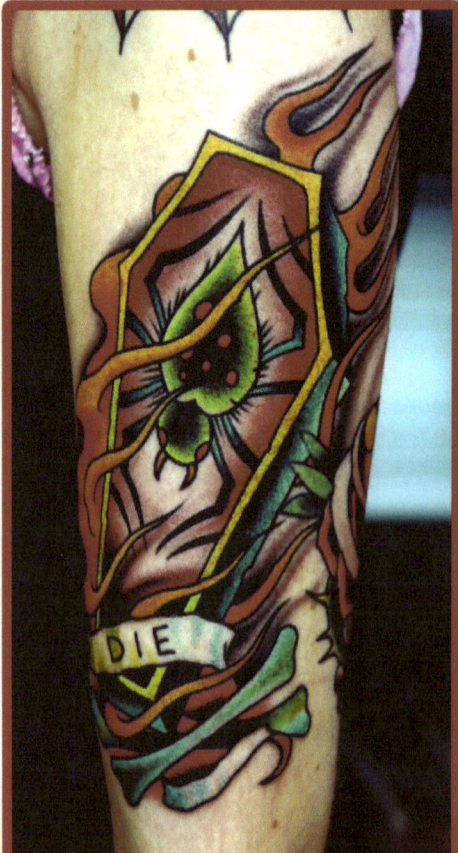

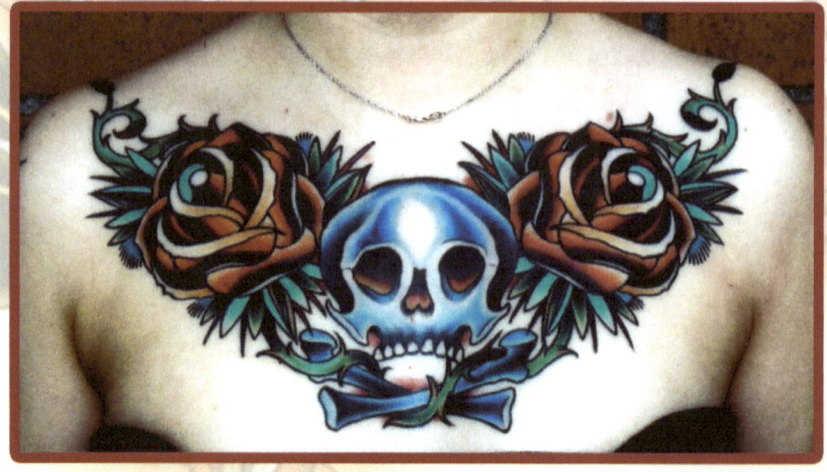

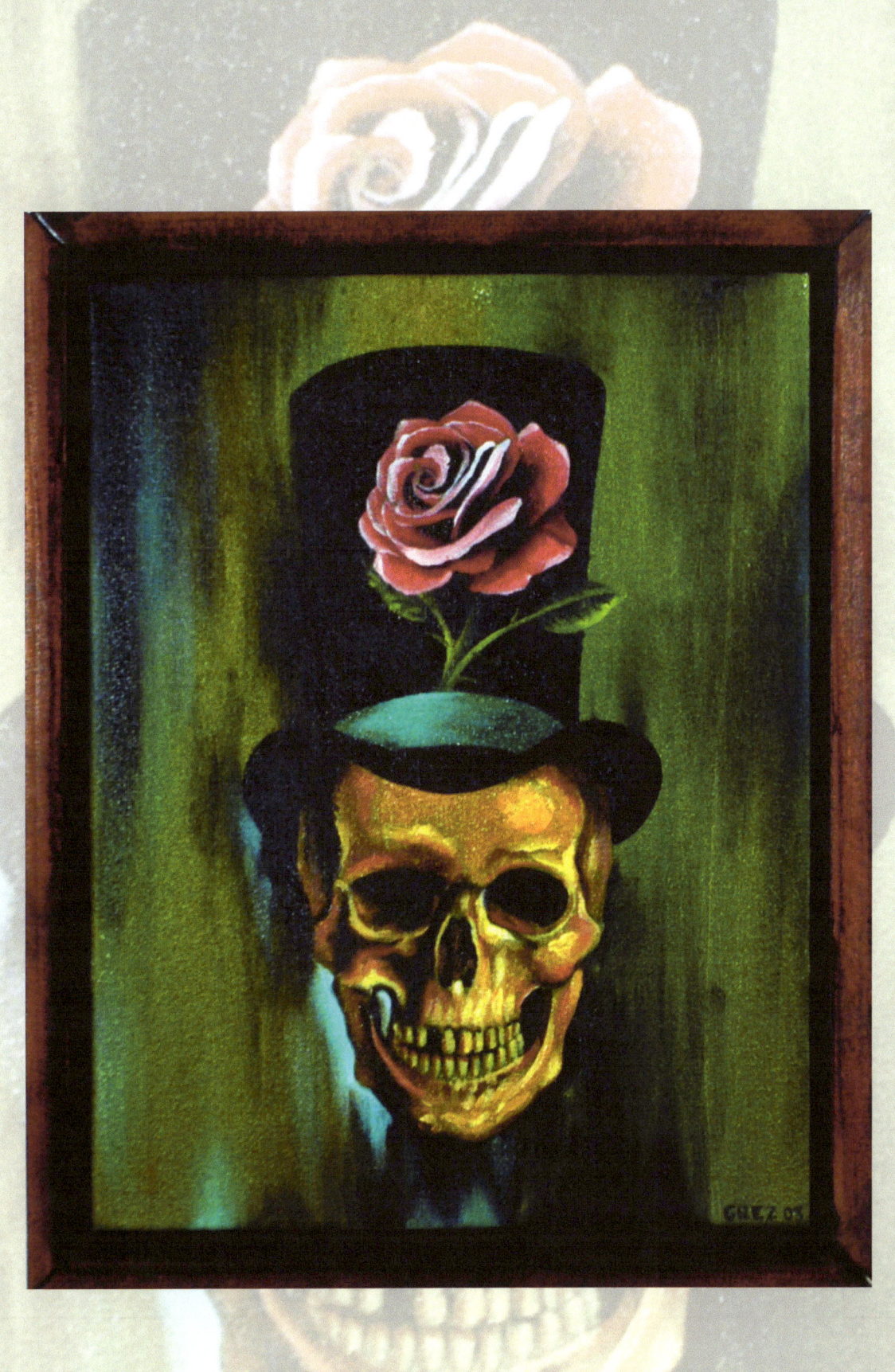

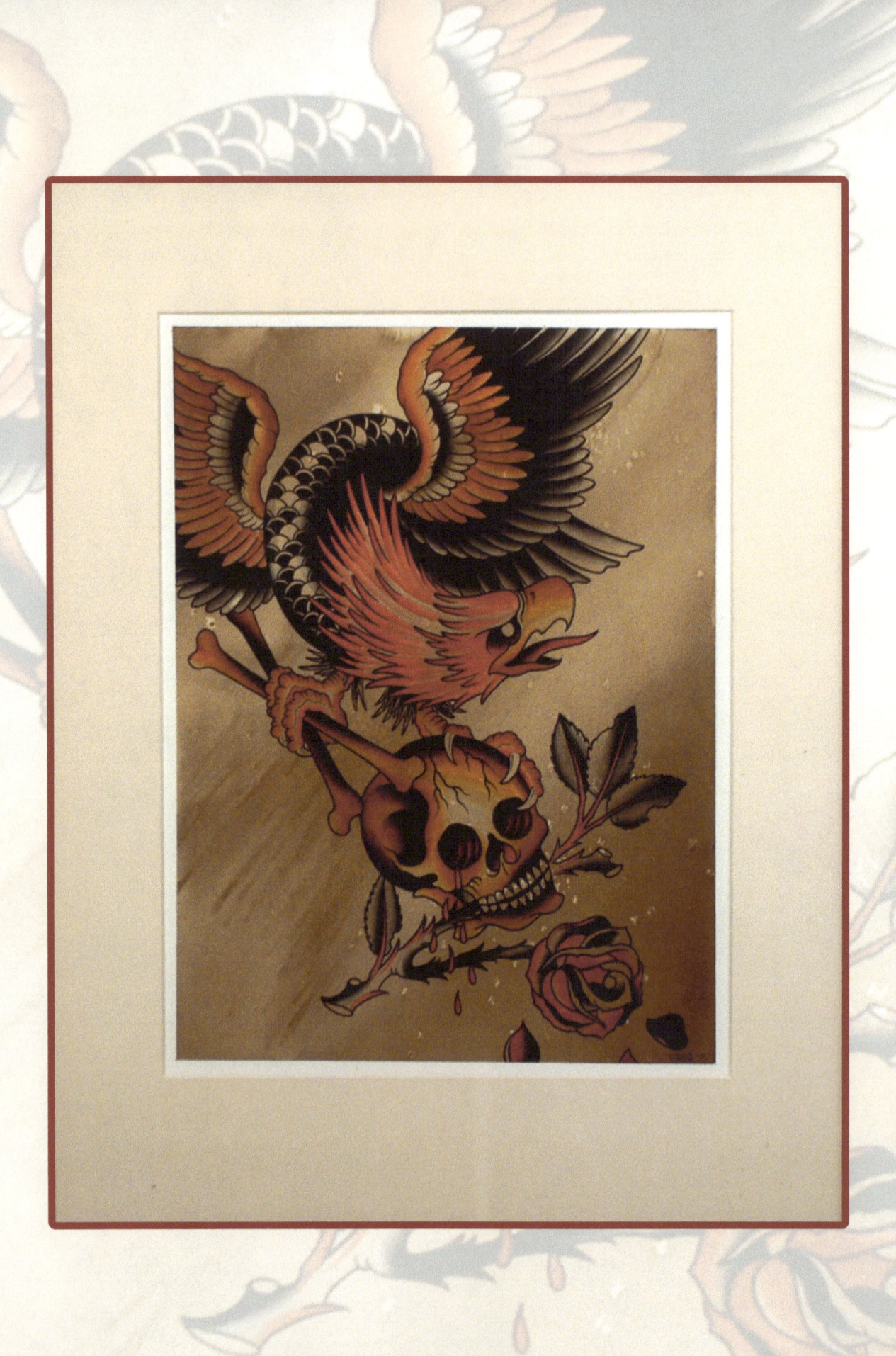

Kore Flatmo

Plura Bella
Appointment only

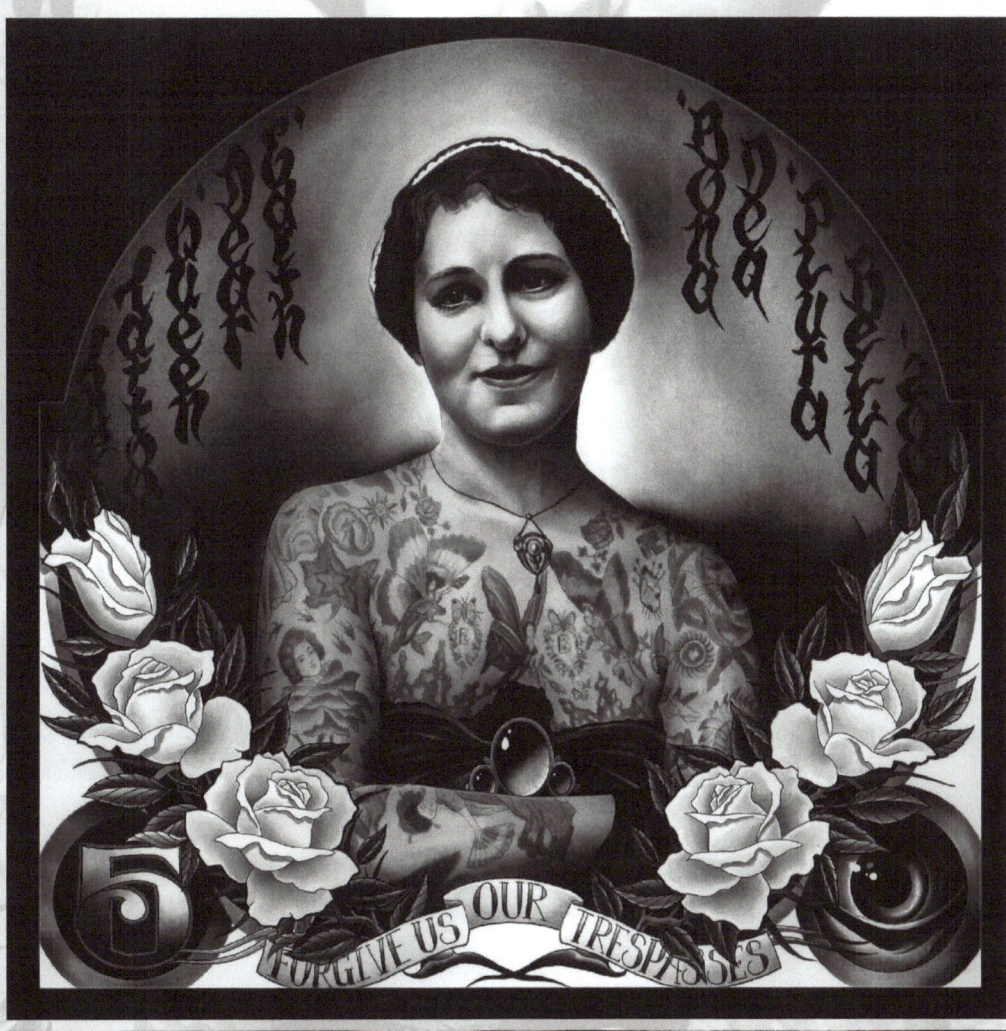

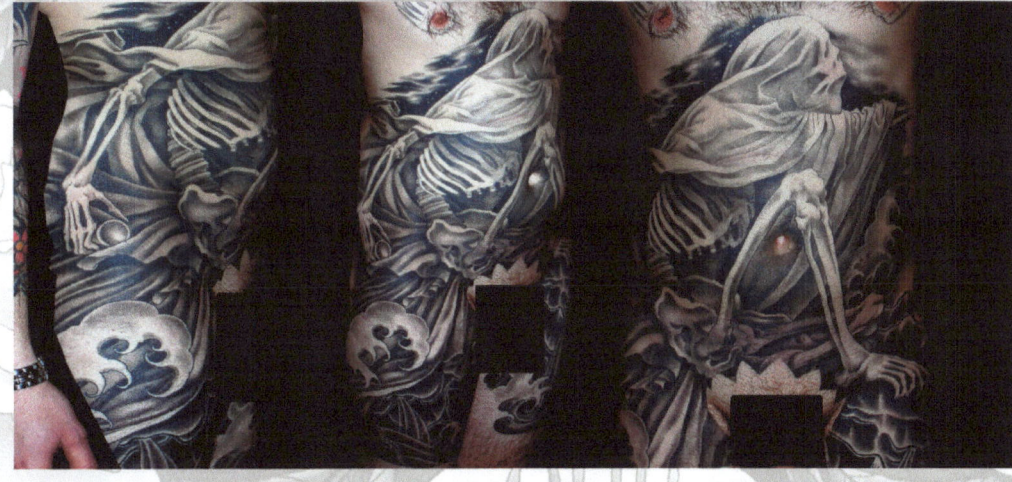

Rob Hiestand

Aces Tattoo 681 S. Virginia St. Reno, NV 89501
(775) 333-0915
www.acestattoo.com

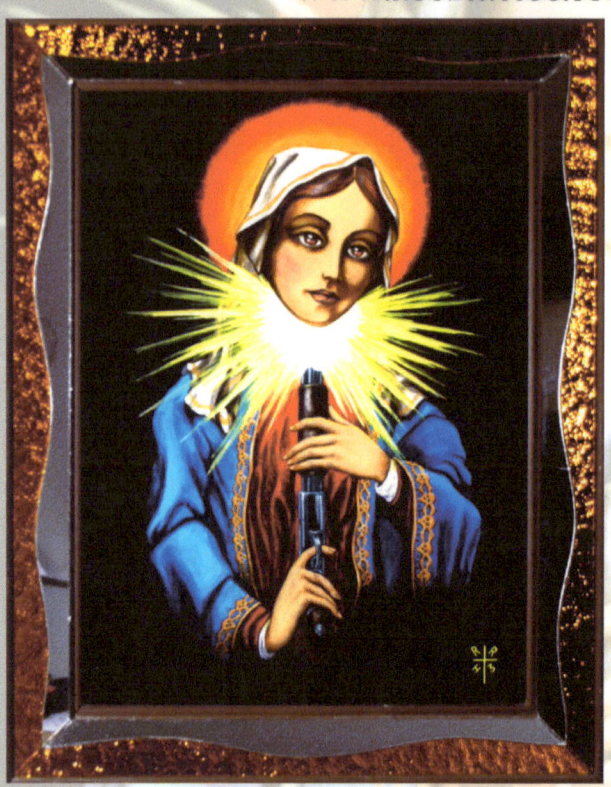
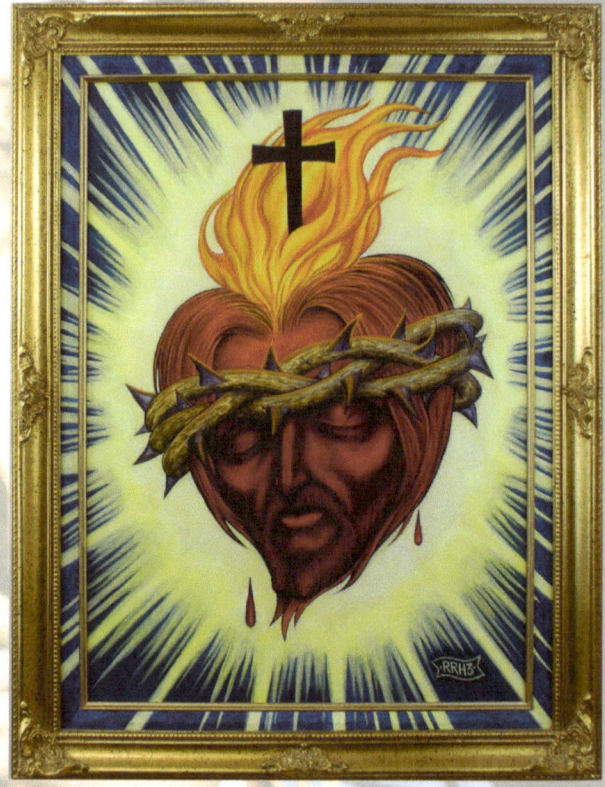
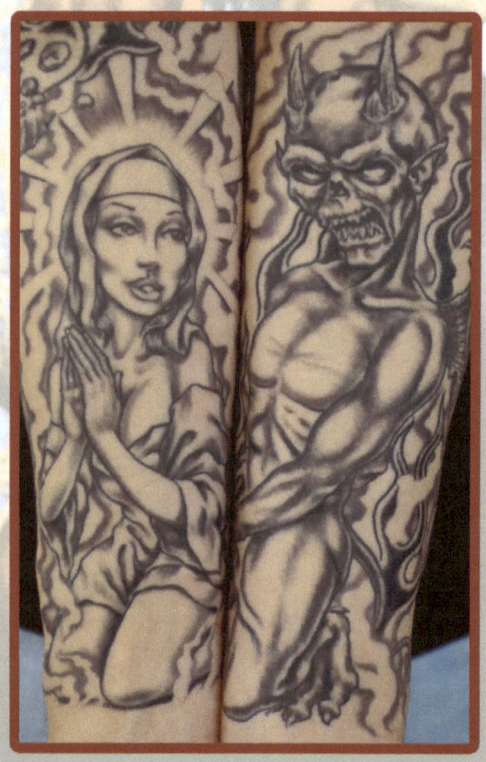

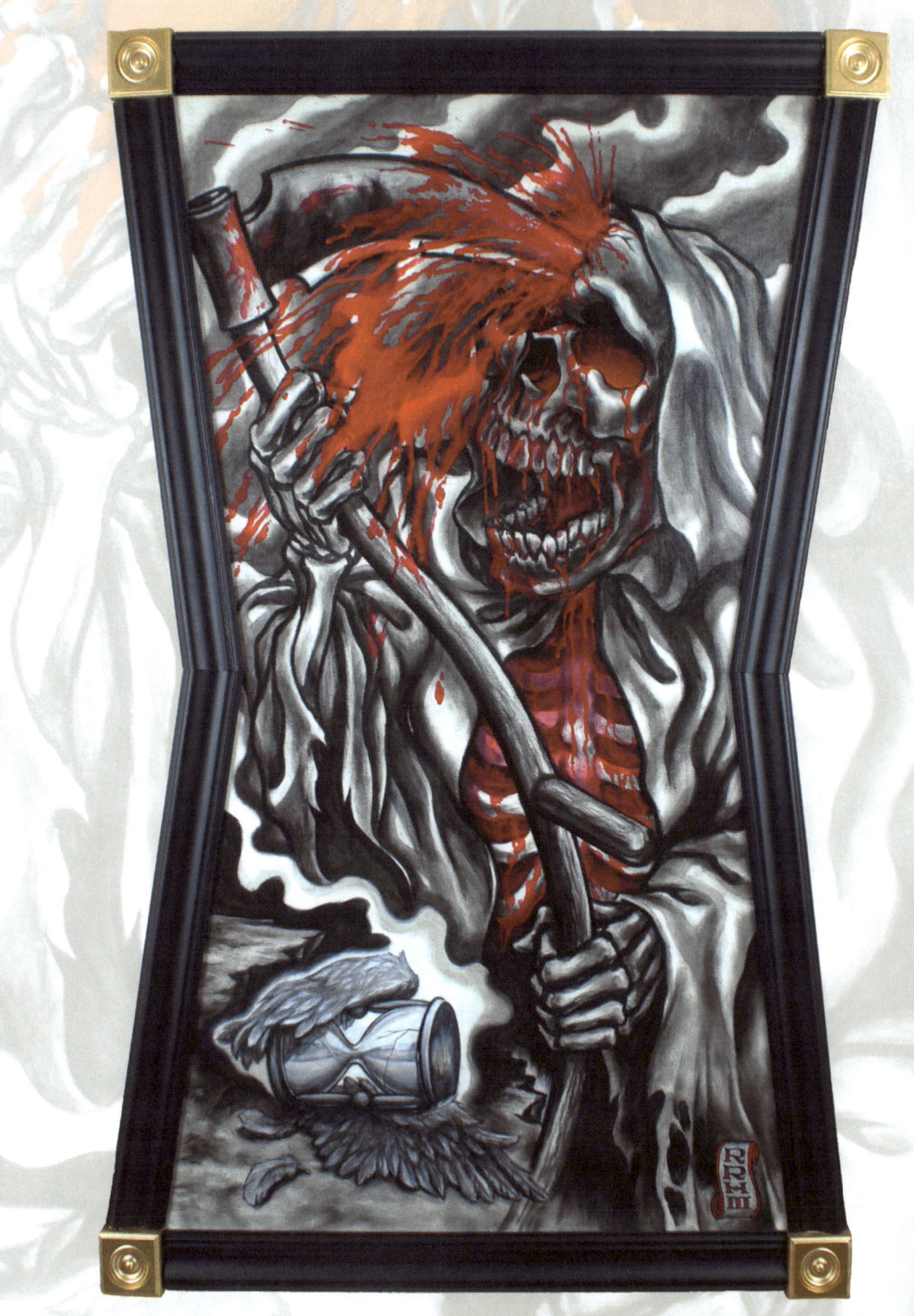

Adam Ciferri

Leviticus Tattoo 4109 E Lake St. Minneapolis, MN
(619) 729-1475
www.leviticustattoo.com

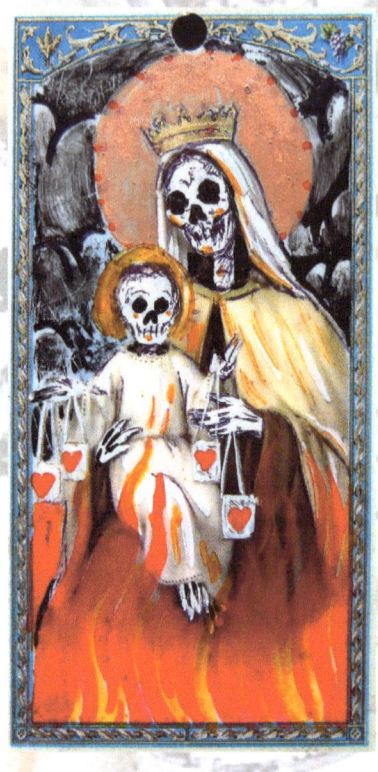

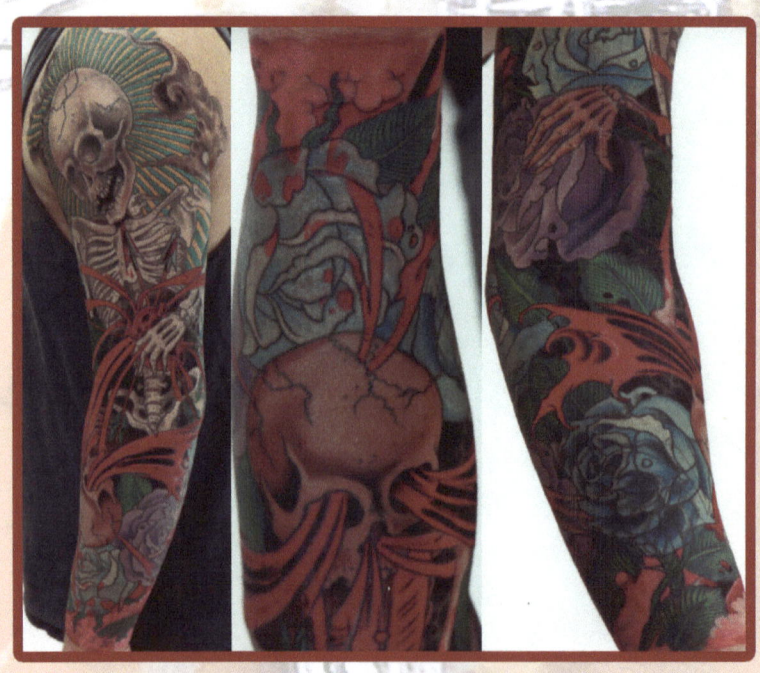

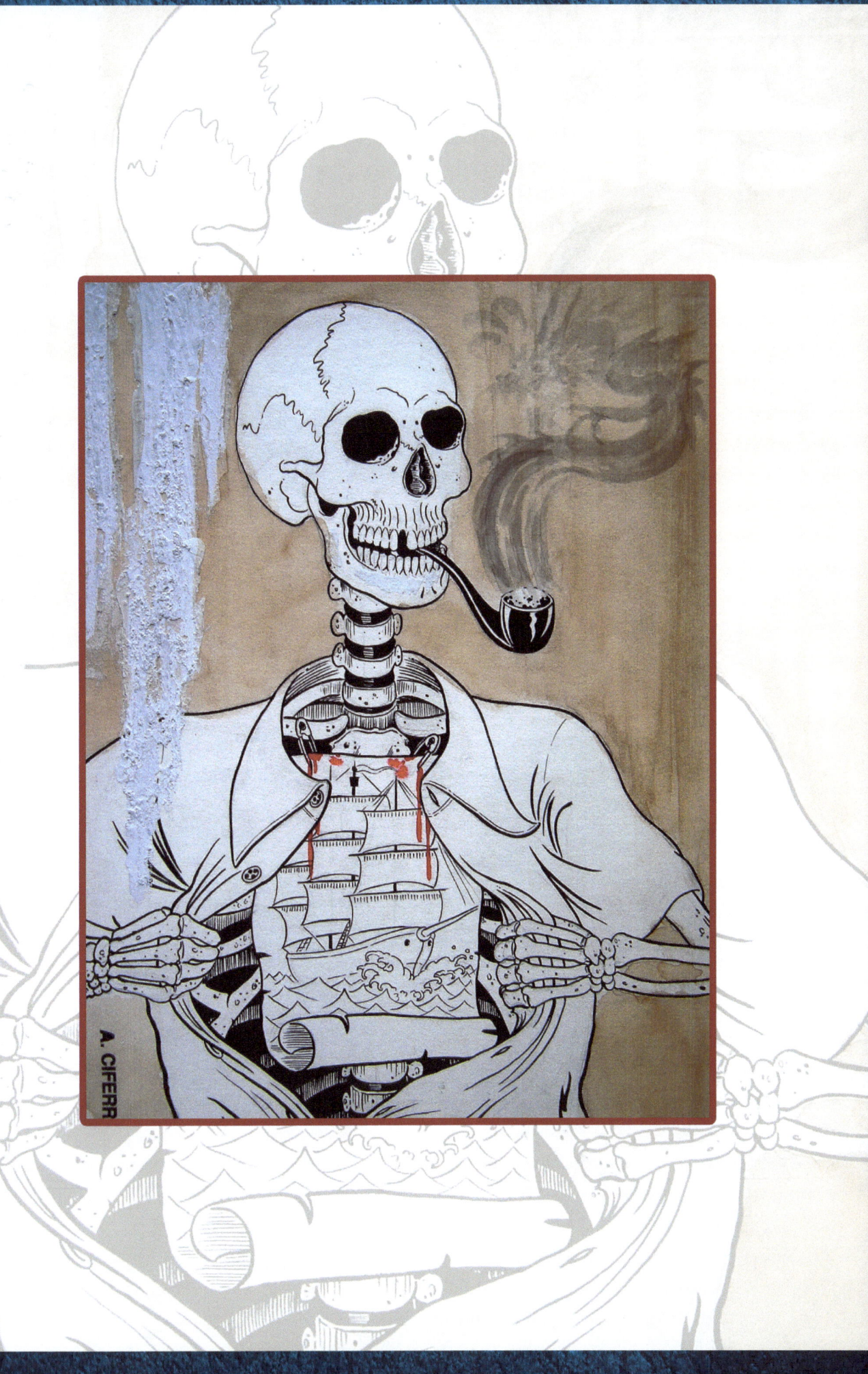

Luke Stewart

Goldfield's Tattoo Studio 404 Broadway San Francisco, CA 94133
(415) 433-0558
www.goldfieldstattoosf.com

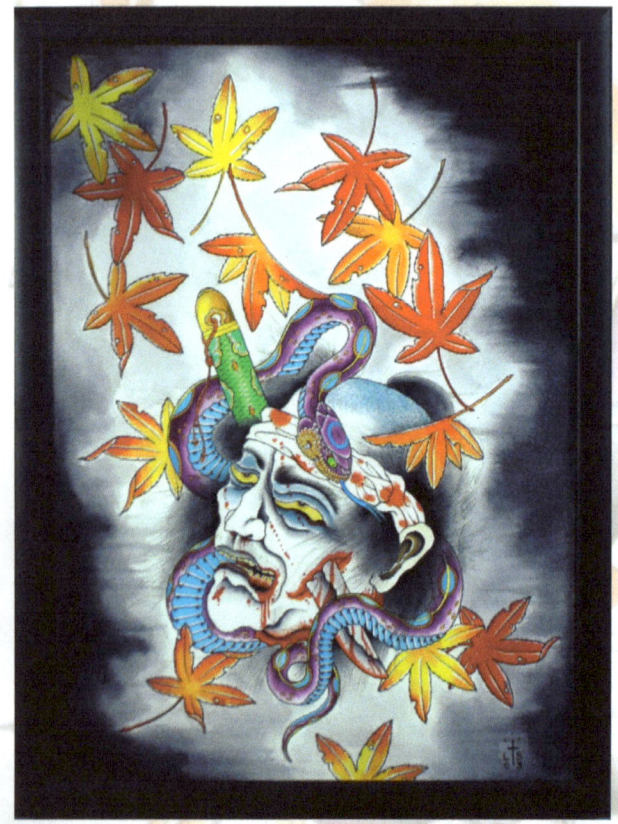

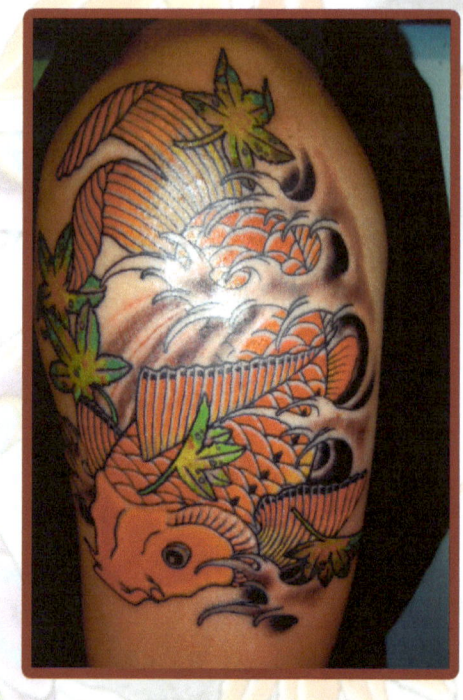

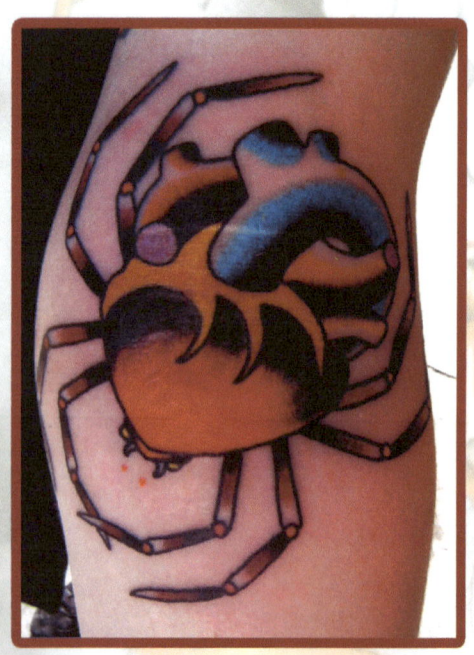

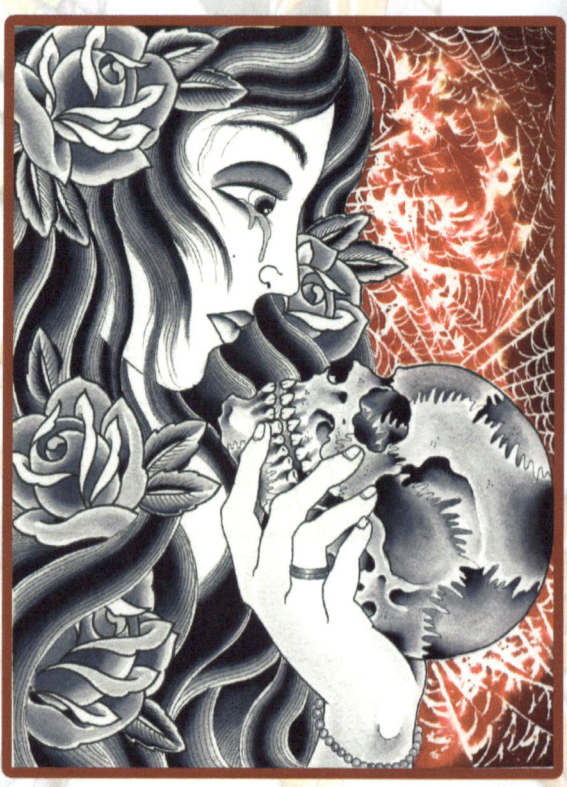

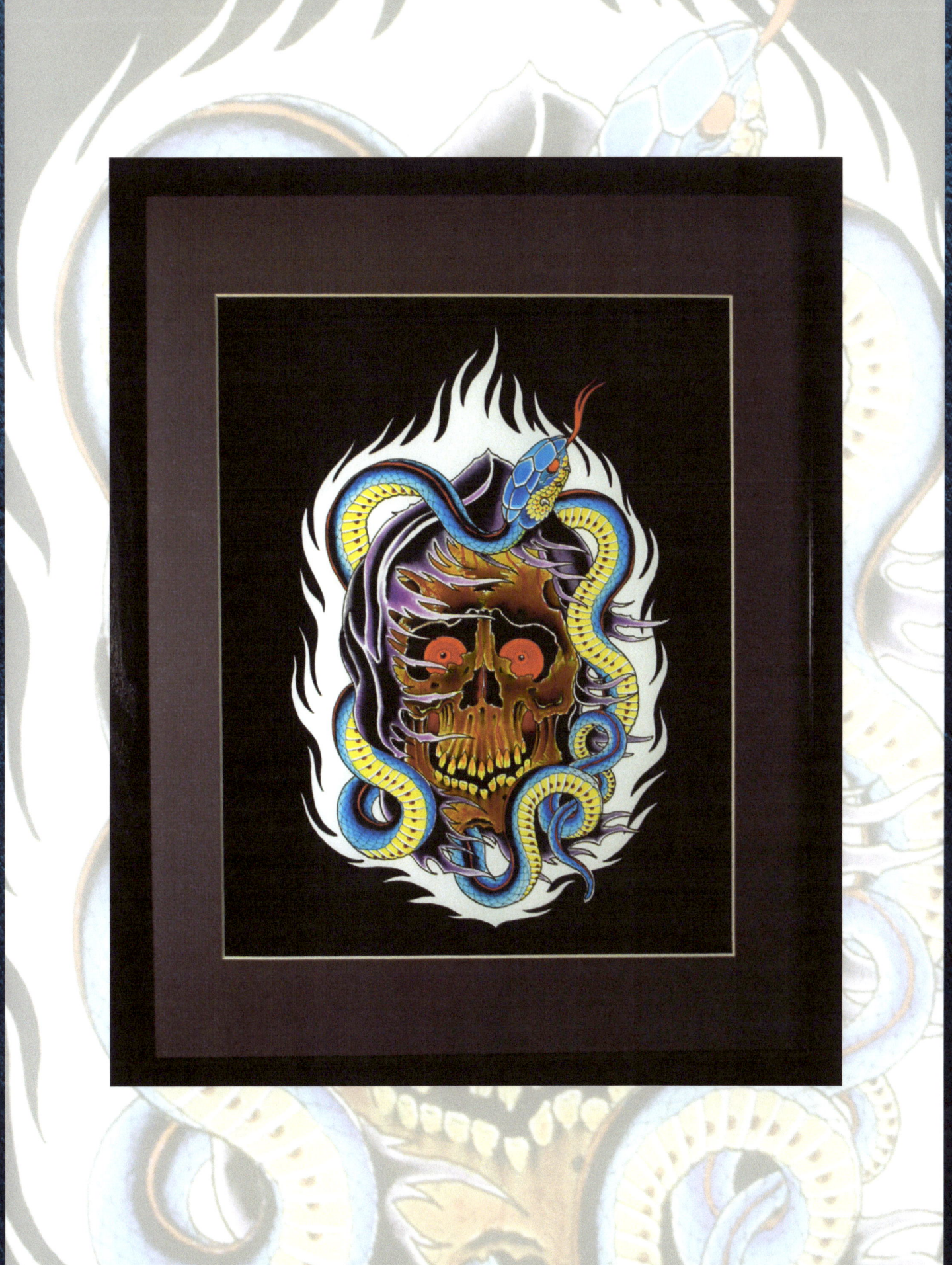

Isaac Fainkujen

No Regrets 806 Ash St Tempe, AZ 85281
(480) 967-5200

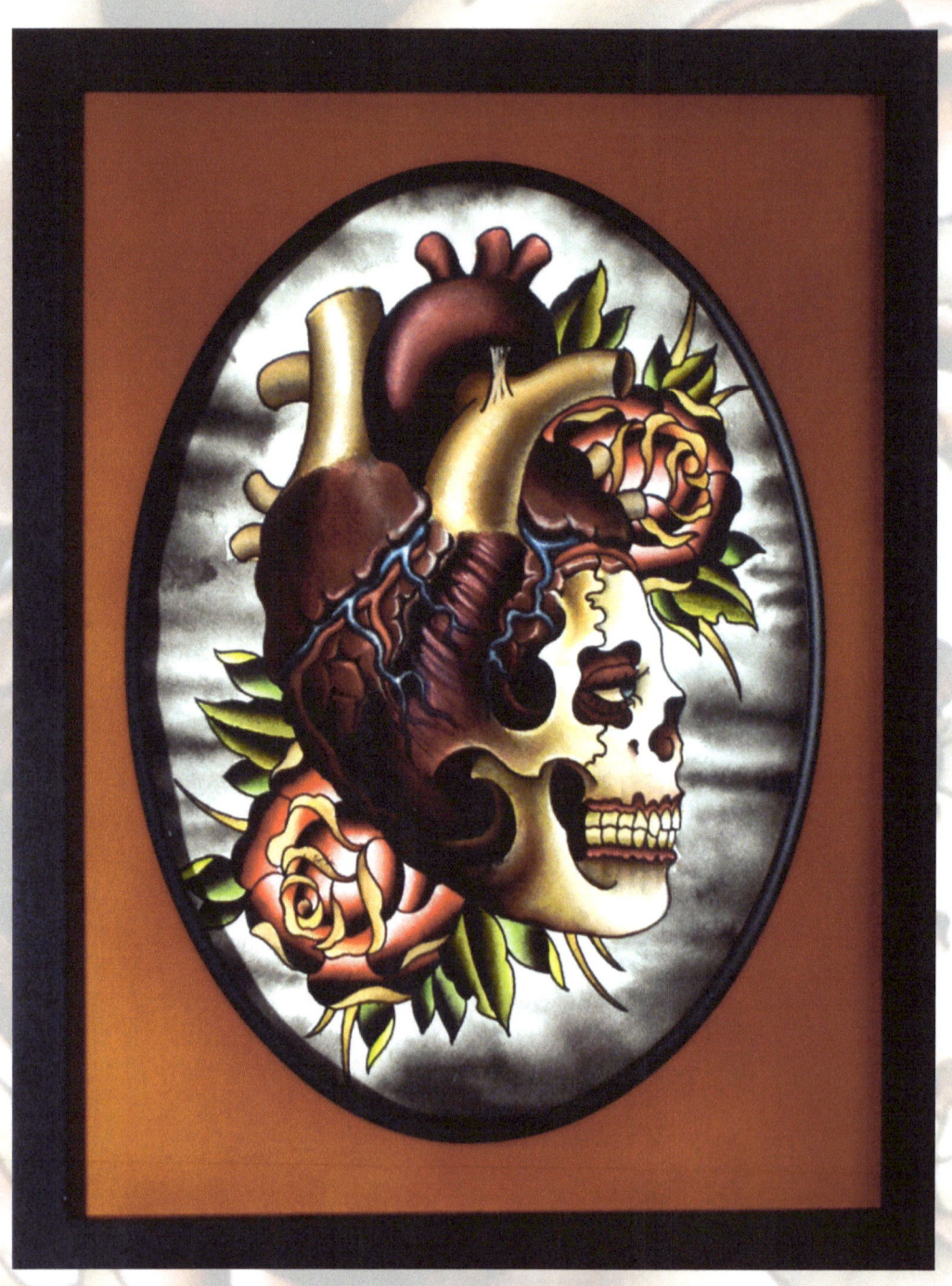

Mike Roper

908 S. Roosevelt Tempe, AZ 85281
By Appointment

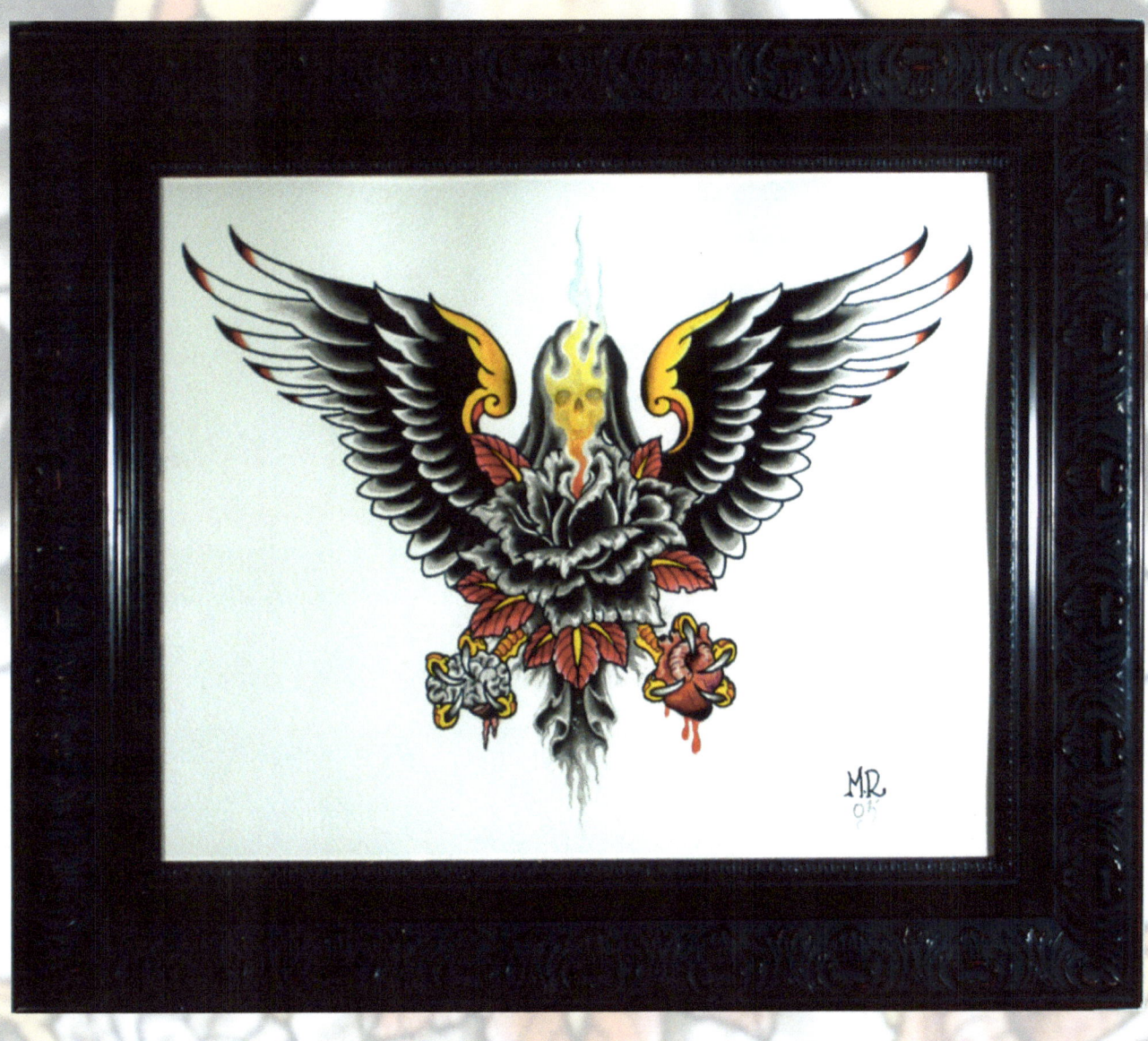

Jared Isenberg

Aces Tattoo 681 S. Virginia St. Reno, NV 89501
(775) 333-0915
www.acestattoo.com

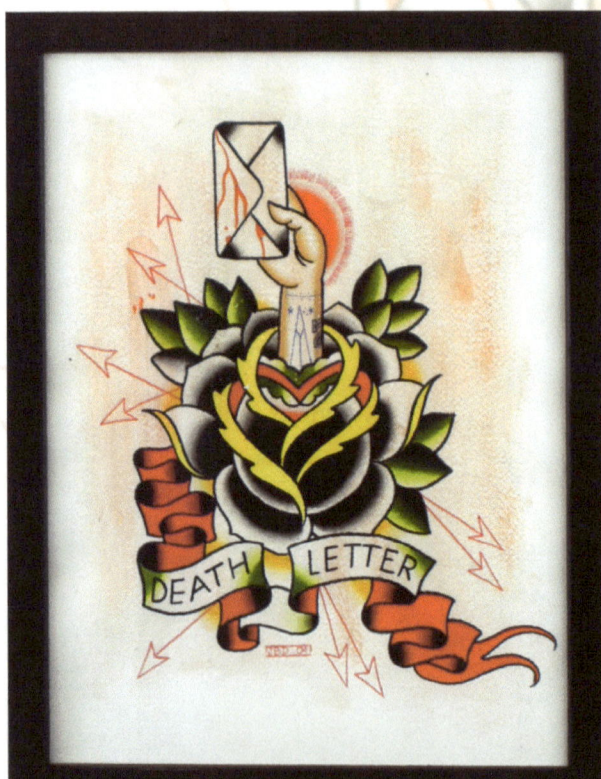

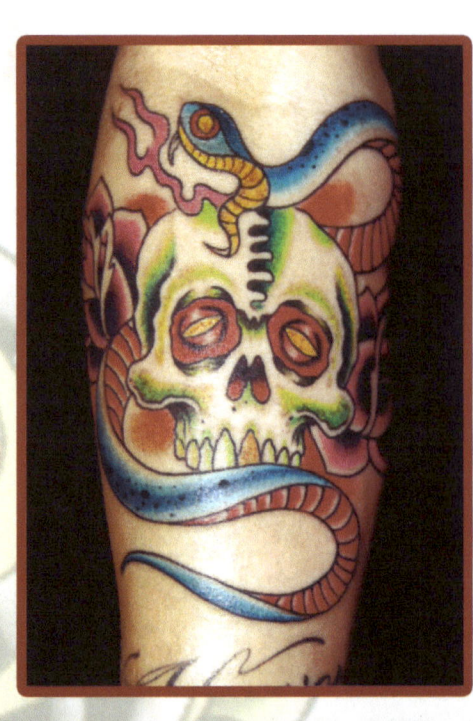

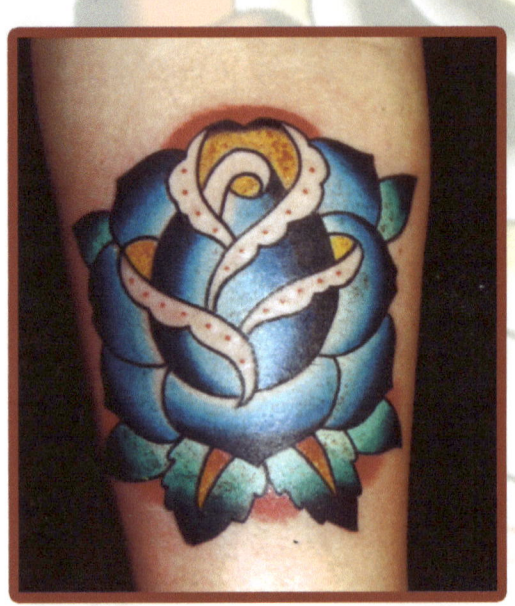

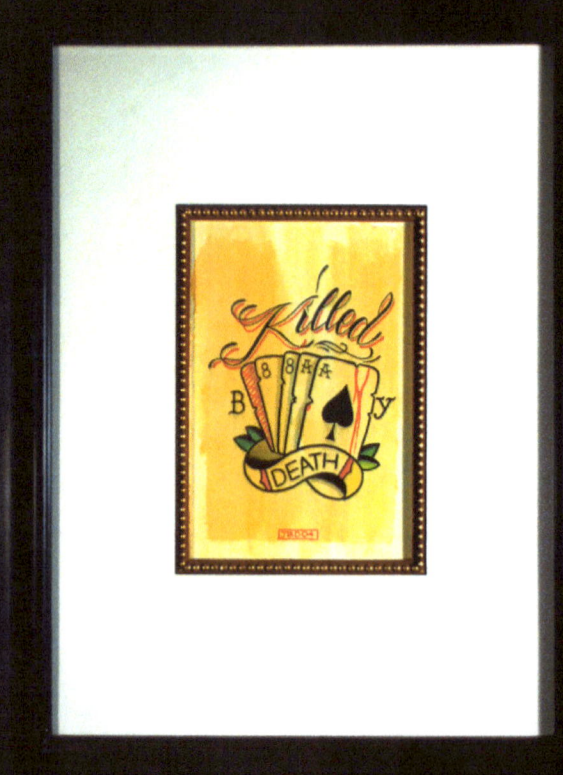

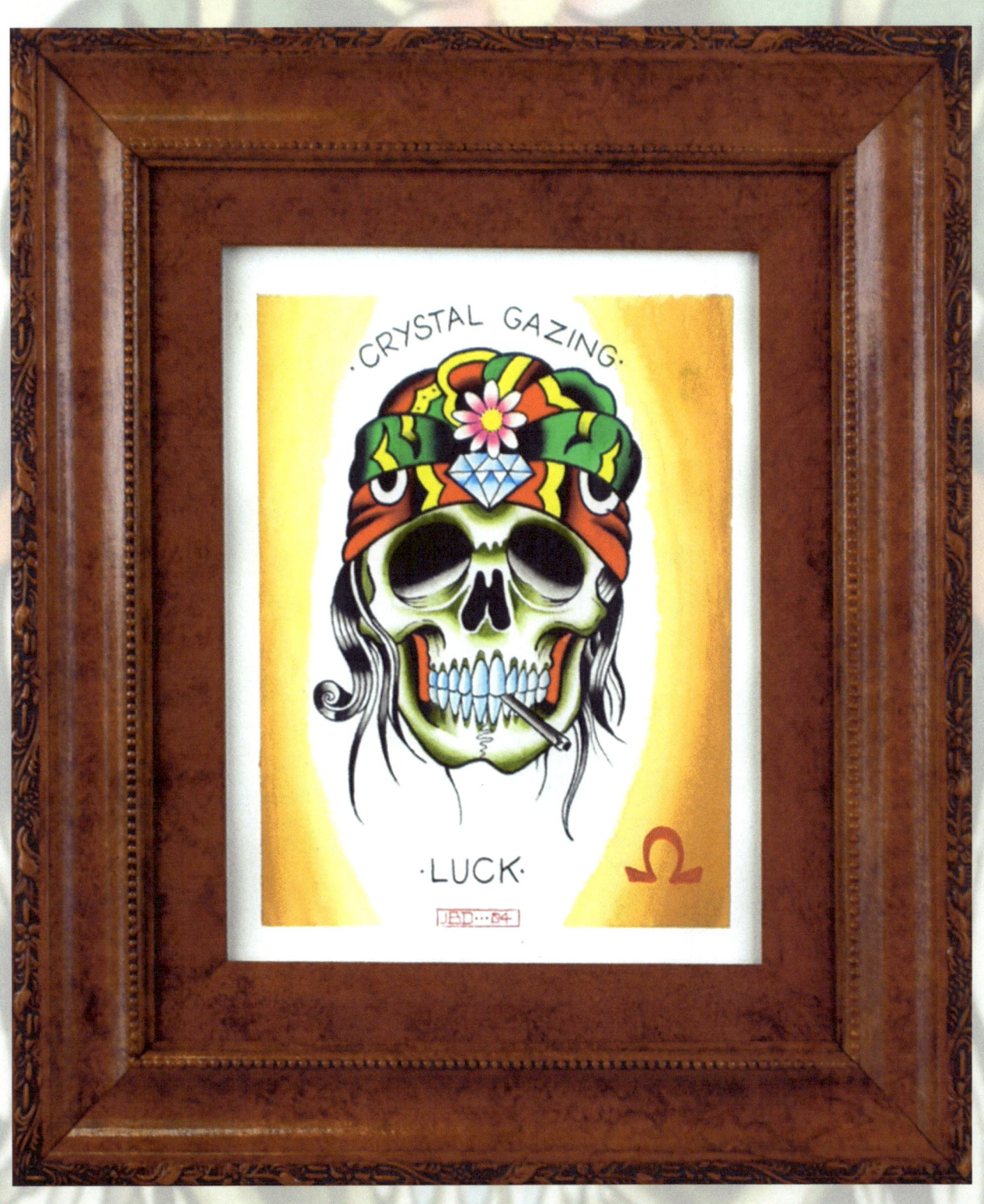

Mike Dorsey

Permanent Productions 129 Calhoun St. Cinci, Oh. 45219
513 281 5800
www.permanetproductions.com

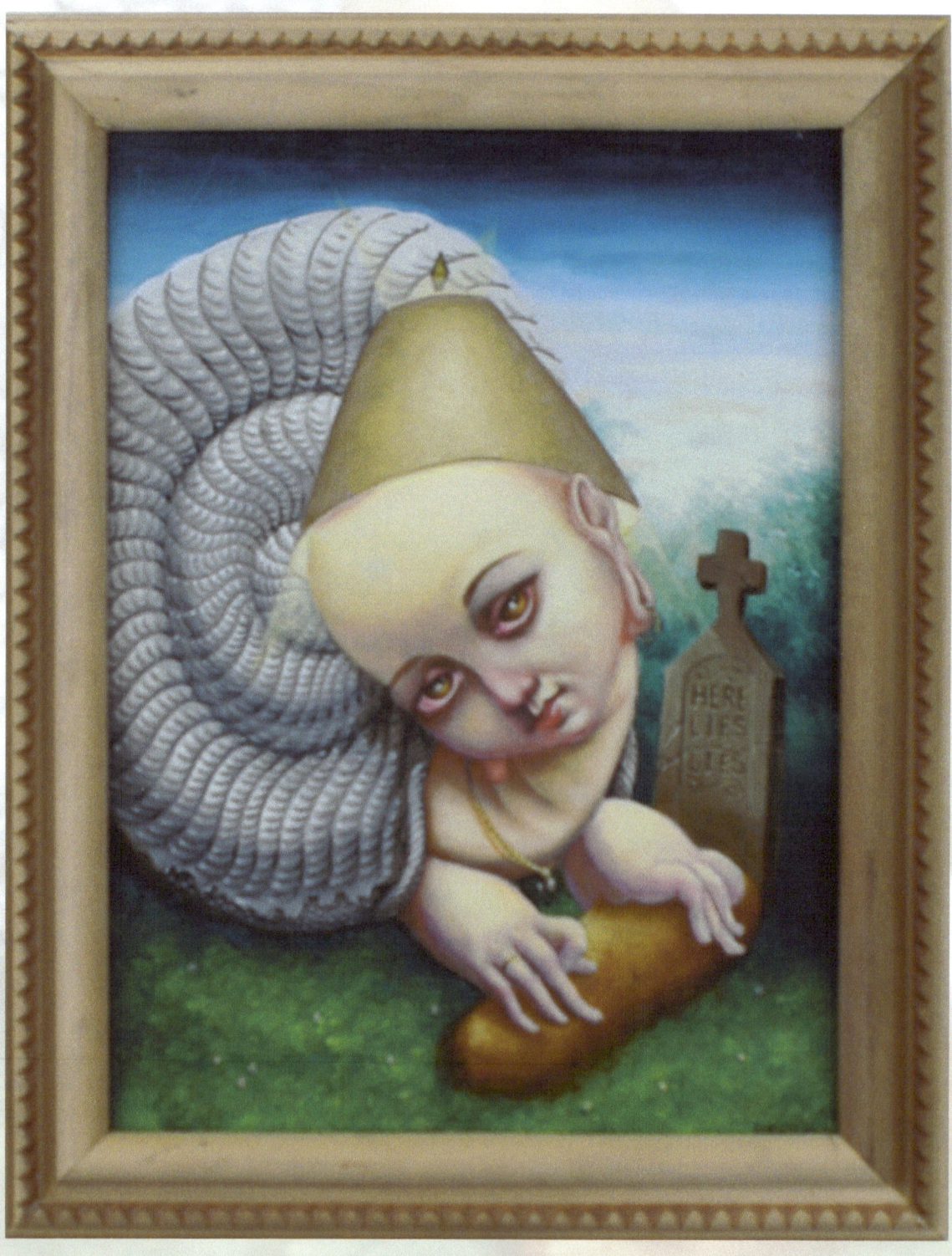

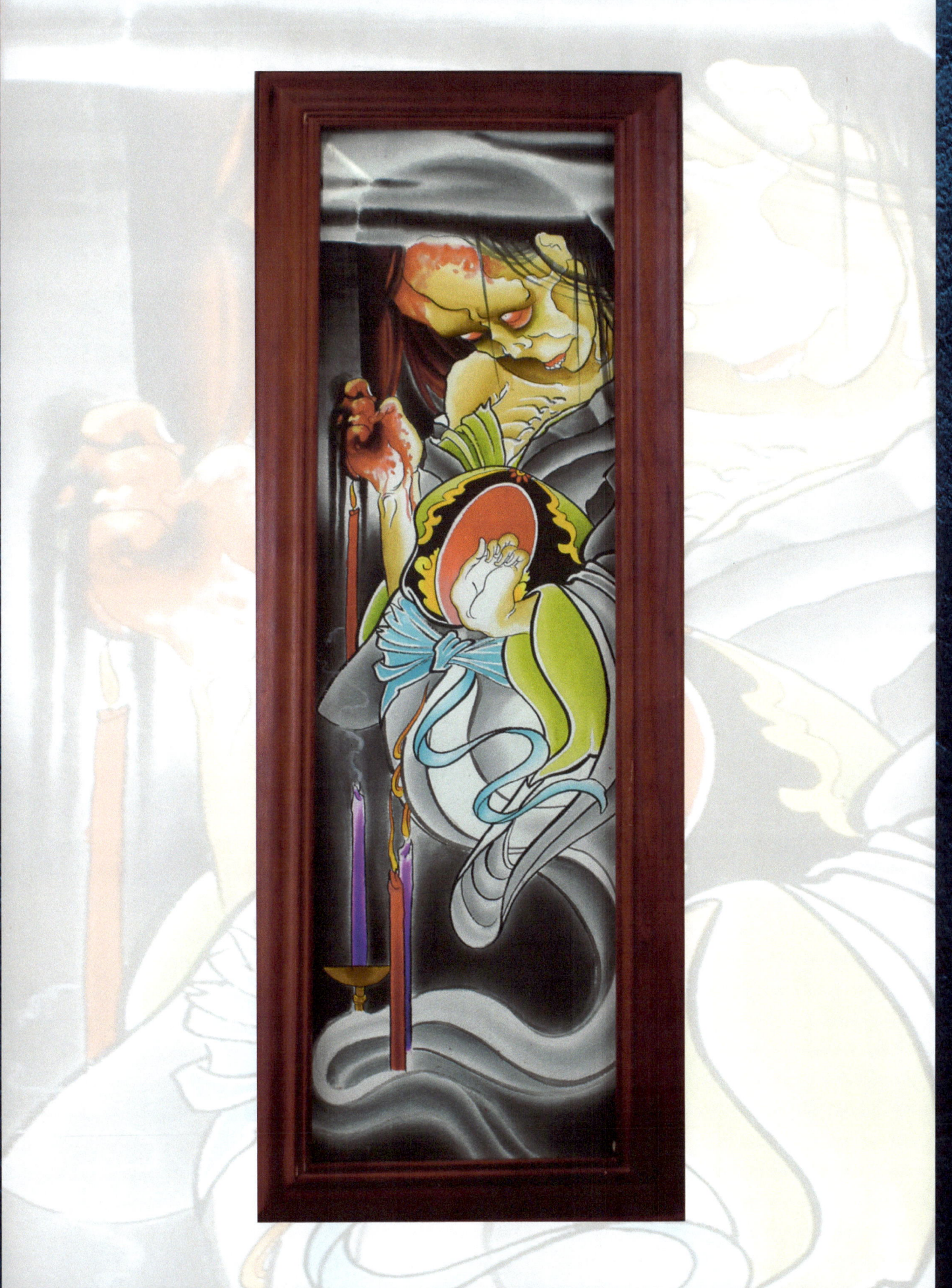

Kurt Melancon

Leviticus Tattoo 4109 E Lake St. Minneapolis, MN 55406
(619) 729-1475
www.leviticustattoo.com

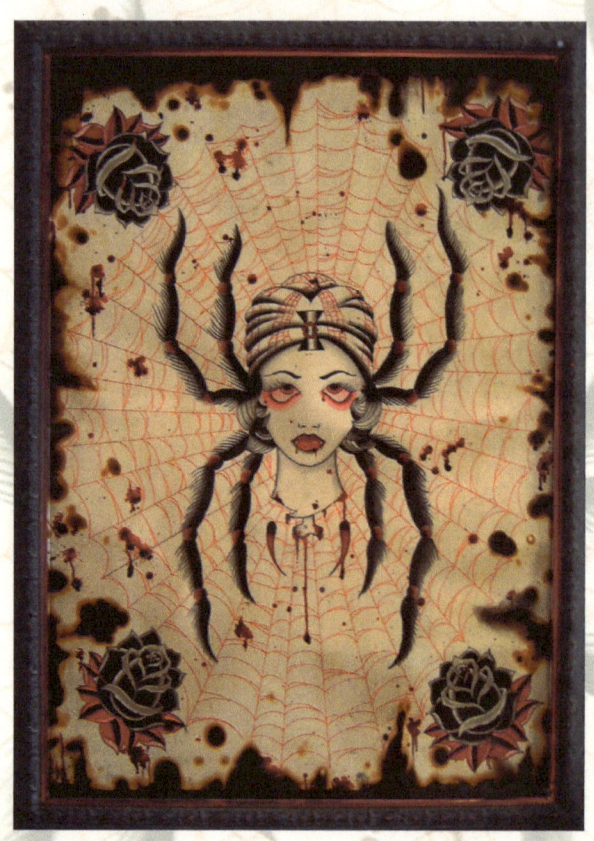

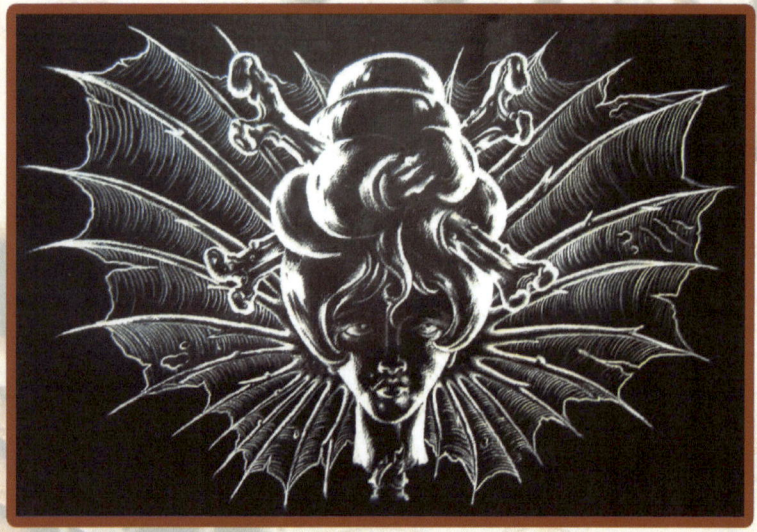

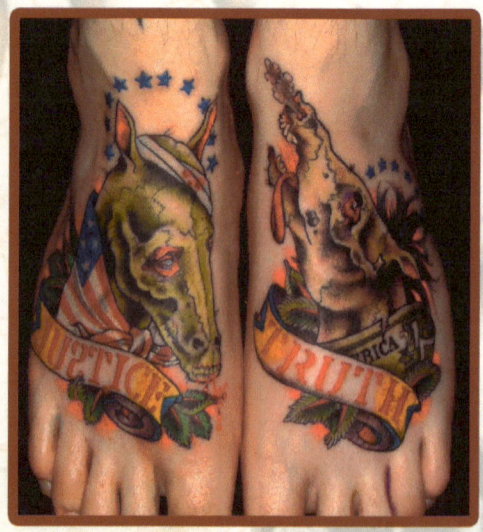

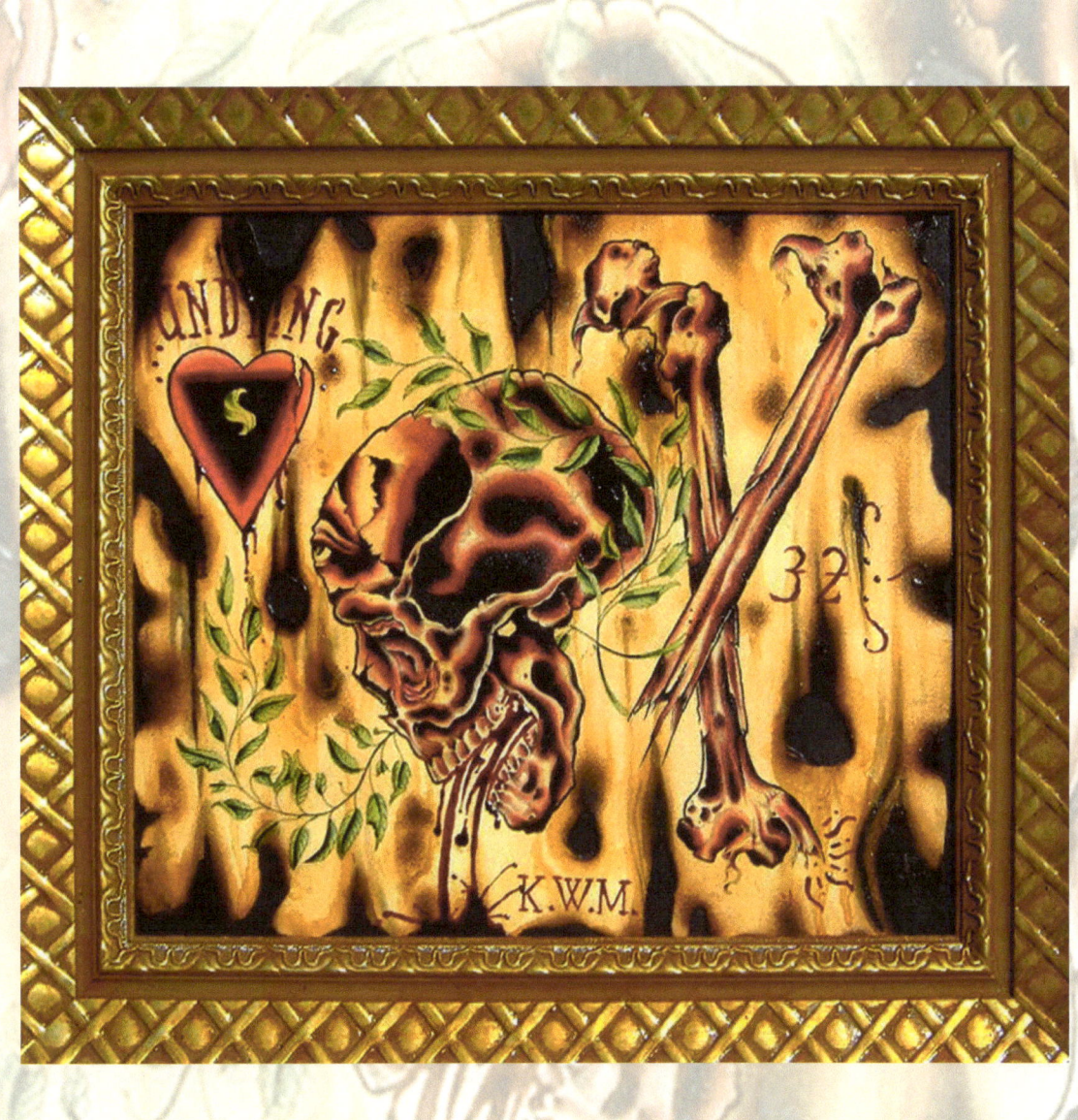

Jason Loui

Redemption Tattoo 2285 Mass. Ave Cambridge, MA 02140
(617) 576-0097
www.redemptiontattoo.com

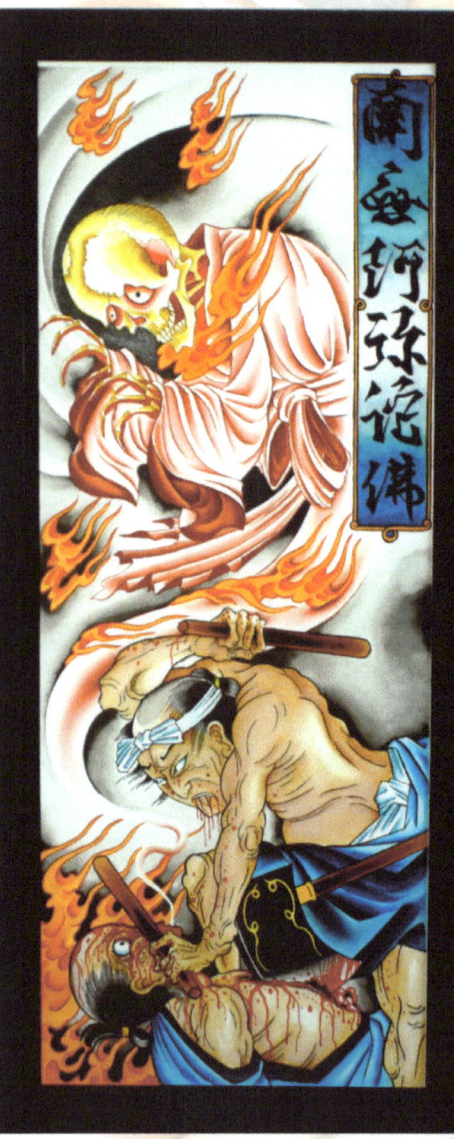
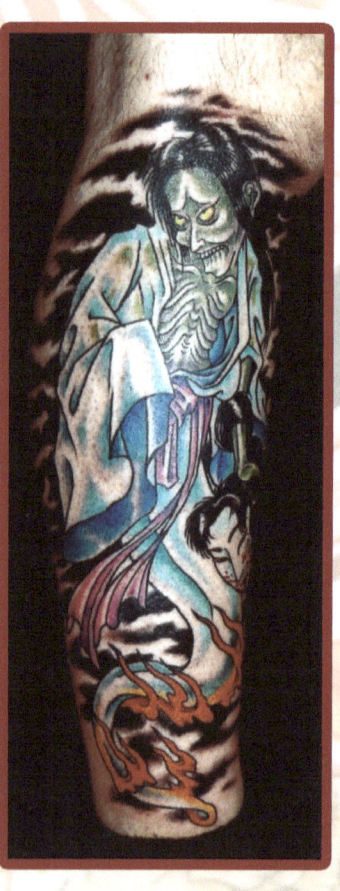
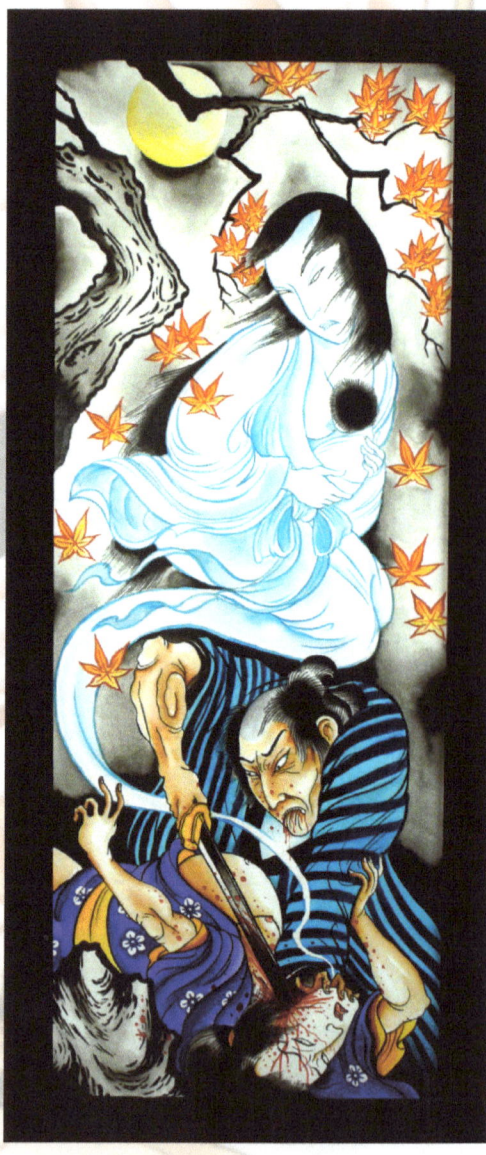

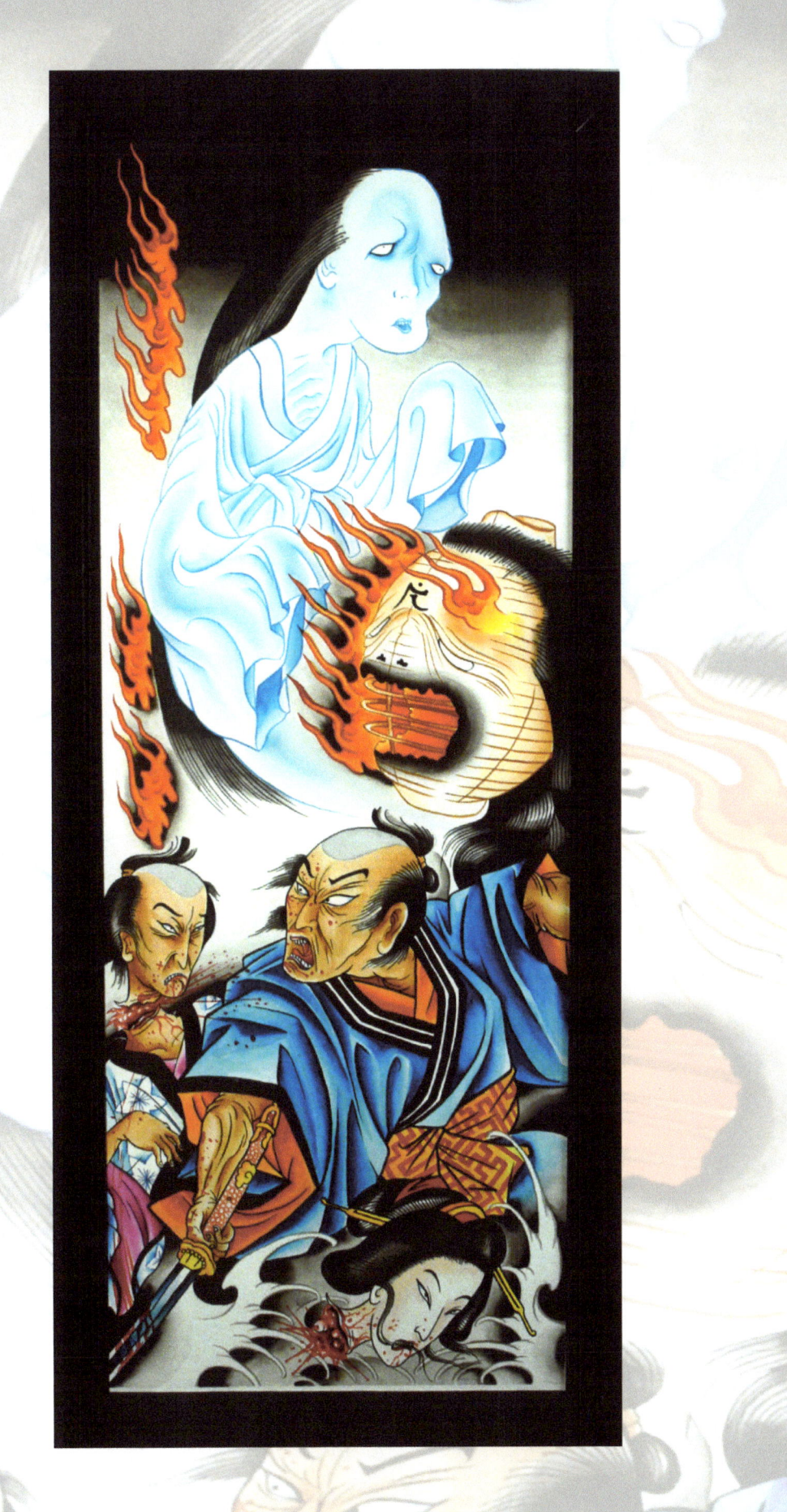

Mike Davis

Everlasting Tattoo
813 Divisadero St, San Francisco, CA 94117
(415) 928-6244
www.everlastingtattoo.com

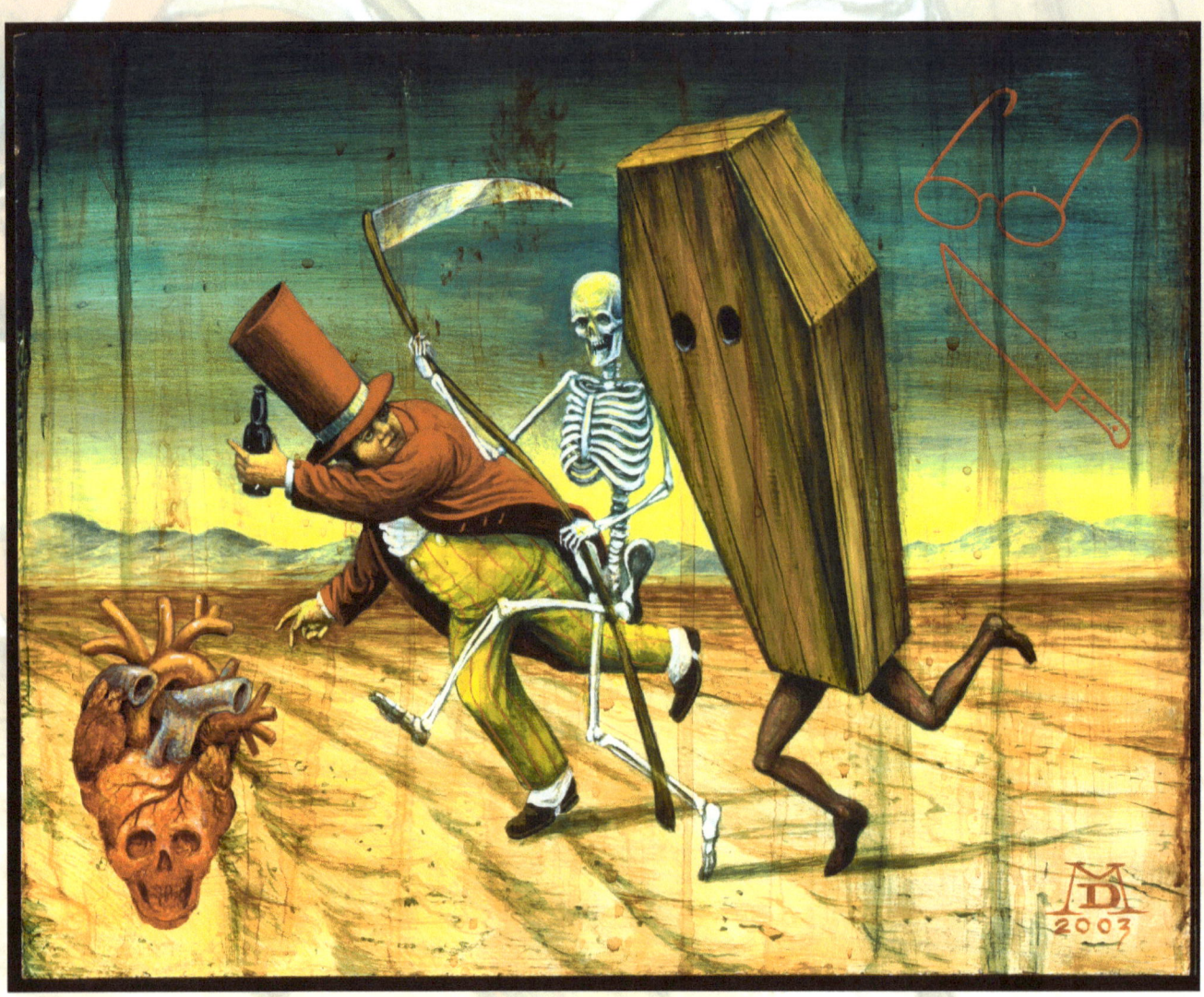

Kevin Cox

Aces Tattoo 681 S. Virginia St. Reno, NV 89501
(775) 333-0915
www.acestattoo.com

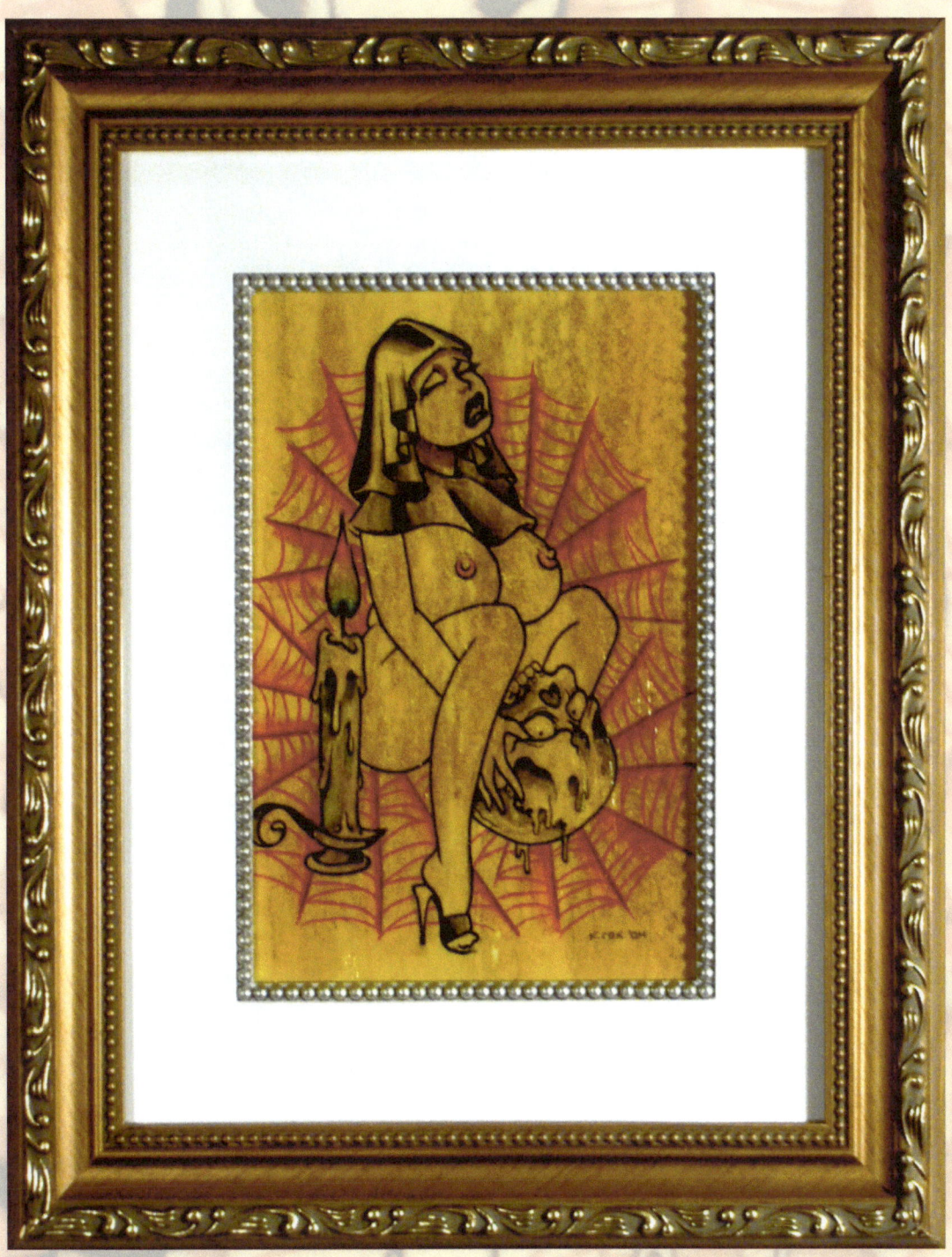

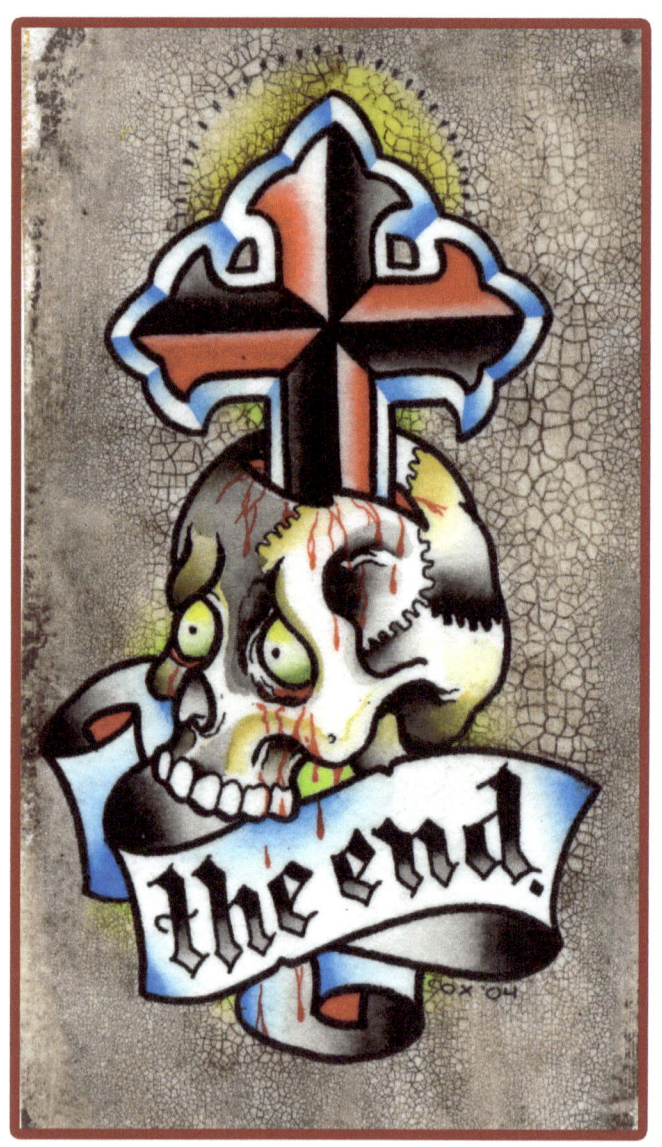

Kevin Cox